Daily life, arts, religion and government of ancient Indian tribes whose development as craftsmen and farmers was ended by drought, erosion and Spanish conquest.

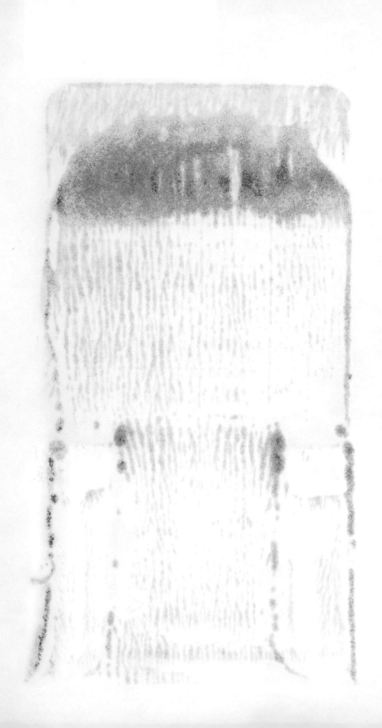

# The
# Ancient Ones

Books by Gordon C. Baldwin

AMERICA'S BURIED PAST
THE WARRIOR APACHE
THE WORLD OF PREHISTORY
THE ANCIENT ONES

# The Ancient Ones

## BASKETMAKERS AND CLIFF DWELLERS OF THE SOUTHWEST

By Gordon C. Baldwin

With an introduction by Dr. Erik K. Reed, Supervisory Archaeologist, National Park Service, U. S. Department of the Interior

W·W·NORTON & COMPANY · INC·
New York

Library of Congress Catalog Card No. 63-11831

Published simultaneously in
Canada by George J. McLeod Limited, Toronto

PRINTED IN THE UNITED STATES OF AMERICA

2 3 4 5 6 7 8 9 0

To Gregg, Linda,
and Blair

# Contents

# Illustrations

— *All photos without credits were taken by the author*

# Acknowledgments

I should like to express my thanks and appreciation to the following individuals and institutions for their cooperation in providing many of the illustrations in this book:

Dr. Emil W. Haury, Director of the Arizona State Museum; Miss Wilma Kaemlein of the Arizona State Museum; Dr. Erik K. Reed, Supervisory Archaeologist, National Park Service; Mrs. Jean M. Pinkley, Park Archaeologist, Mesa Verde National Park; Gordon Vivian and Sallie Van Valkenburgh of the Southwest Archaeological Center.

I should also like to thank Patricia P. Paylore, Assistant Librarian, University of Arizona, for permitting me access to the University of Arizona Library; Dale Stuart King for the loan of numerous books; Dr. Erik K. Reed for reference material; and my wife, Pauline Baldwin, for endless patience and the thankless task of typing the final manuscript.

# Introduction

In this book, Dr. Gordon C. Baldwin examines the field he knows best, the subject in which both he and I have been specialists for some thirty years, the southwestern United States, a region of special fascination both geographically and archaeologically. The northern part of the Southwest particularly has always aroused interest and appealed to the imagination. This is the region of the Navaho Reservation and surrounding areas; the "Four Corners country" of northeastern Arizona, southeasternmost Utah, southwesternmost Colorado, and northwestern New Mexico. It is a high arid land of mesas and canyons, of mountains and cliffs, of bare red rock and of dry watercourses. It is primarily the range, in recent times, of the picturesque Navaho Indians — who are not the descendants of the ancient folk Dr. Baldwin describes. Not related to the Pueblos, the Navaho is a very different kind of Indian, a comparative newcomer to the Southwest, and an even more recent arrival in the present Navaho country.

Until very recently the Navaho country was largely remote, difficult of access, undisturbed by modern progress and contemporary technological civilization. Things are different now, changing rapidly, with a network of paved roads extending across most sections of the region. But within Dr. Baldwin's and my recollection, much of the area was a problem, occasionally an adventure, to reach; and travelers through it were few.

No matter how much development occurs, however, and no matter how many other people are traveling through at high speed on good roads — the spectacular, often fantastic, plateau scenery cannot lose its impact and inspiration, nor the cliff dwellings and other ancient ruins their grip on the imagination. It still is possible to step back 700 years by rounding a bend in a canyon to reach a long-abandoned pueblo in a shallow cave under a sandstone cliff.

In this book, Dr. Baldwin describes the cultural history of the Pueblo Indians — tells the story of the ruins and of the objects found in them, interpreting this raw material into a continuous narrative of human life in the semi-arid plateau environment.

The story opens 2,000 years ago or more, with an early simple people living scattered in small groups across the country. They were not much further along, at first, on the path toward civilization than the Australian aborigines. But in addition to hunting large and small animals and gathering edible wild plants, they were already raising a little corn by the time we first pick up their traces in the archaeological record. Farming had begun, in a small way — the decisive first major step toward settled life in permanent communities and consequent development of civilization. At first, however, they were not far removed from the wandering life of the hunting folk with minimum equipment. Nevertheless, they had already brought certain arts and crafts to a high peak — notably basketry, and hence they are called the Basketmakers.

Dr. Baldwin recounts how these people received and developed successive additions to their cultural inventory — improvements in their way of life — such as permanent houses, pottery-making, stone axes, the bow and arrow, the hard cradle board, domestication of the wild turkey, and additional crops including squash, beans, and cotton. More important than any one specific item is the general change of pattern — to sedentary life and large villages. Upon the completion of this transition from the Basketmaker way of living, about 1200 years ago, the people of the Four Corners region have become clearly recognizable as Pueblos, direct ancestors of the modern Pueblo Indians of New Mexico and the Hopi country. As Dr. Baldwin points out, there was no change of population — no invasion or immigration of any consequence. The earlier Basketmakers were equally the direct ancestors of the Pueblo Indians.

Many archaeologists use the term Anasazi to refer to both the Basketmakers and their Pueblo descendants together. Dr. Baldwin also does this occasionally. I rather like the sound, and the significance, of "Anasazi" — it is a Navaho word or phrase meaning, approximately, "ancient enemies." The implication is misleading, for the Navaho Indians reached the present Navaho country long after its abandonment by the Anasazi, But the idea adds to the romantic effect of the ruins. However, they are sufficiently fascinating and exciting without this additional detail — especially the cliff dwellings of the thirteenth century, and the great pueblos in the open such as those of Chaco Canyon.

Describing the fully developed Pueblo culture of the classic period, Dr. Baldwin rightly emphasizes these major sites and the local regional variations, but also brings out the broad unity of Anasazi culture and the interrelationships between different areas. We then reach a problem far more controversial than any of the several minor puzzles in the earlier part of the story — why did they disappear? Dr. Baldwin discusses the various theories in explanation of the Anasazi abandonment of the San Juan River drainage about 1300 A.D. and then goes on to point out that they did not actually disappear as a group but moved into other areas where Pueblo Indians continued living — including those of the present. He also points out that the late pre-Spanish period, 1300-1540, was one of climax and high achievement in many ways in the areas where Pueblo occupation continued. Finally he treats of the Spanish conquest in the sixteenth century, the history of the Indians under Spanish rule, and the living Pueblos of the present day.

And so this is a story not only of mysterious antiquities from the buried past in remote wilderness regions, but also of live human beings and of the immediate ancestors of contemporary fellow citizens. It is the story of the background and the achievements of one segment of modern America.

ERIK K. REED
Supervisory Archaeologist
National Park Service
U.S. Department of the Interior

# The
# Ancient Ones

# 1
# Cliff Dwellings and Chindi

"Ye-e-a-a-a-oh."

The blood-curdling scream brought my eyes wide open, staring upward through the night's blackness. Faint starlight filtered in through the square opening overhead, vaguely outlining rough log beams and closely spaced cross poles. It was well after midnight, I judged.

Beside me dry leaves rustled as Louis Caywood sat up on our blanket bed.

"What was that awful racket?" Louis wanted to know, his voice thick with sleep.

"Sounded like someone's in trouble," I said. "Let's have a look."

Because of the cool night air we hadn't removed any clothing before going to bed, and it took only a few moments to slip into our shoes. One after the other we hoisted ourselves up through the hatchway to the top. Side by side we stood at the edge of the cliff dwelling's flat roof and looked around.

Louis and I were members of a University of Arizona summer archaeological field school exploring prehistoric

Fig. 1. Betatakin cliff ruin in northern Arizona.

ruins in northern Arizona. After a long six-mile hike up
Segie Canyon from Marsh Pass, where we had left our cars,
we had camped for the night in the 700-year-old cliff dwelling of Betatakin, meaning Hillside House.

After supper, we built up the campfire and Dr. Byron
Cummings told us something about the ruin and its former
inhabitants. We couldn't have had a better teacher. Back in
1909 Dr. Cummings had discovered Betatakin and, during
the following 23 years, he had discovered and excavated
hundreds of other prehistoric cliff dwellings and pueblos
throughout Arizona and southern Utah. Now past 70 years
of age, he could still outdig and outwalk most of his students.

Perhaps you are wondering why archaeologists are so
interested in cliff dwellings. In short, why dig up broken
pots and dead Indians? What good is it in today's atomic
age?

That night around the campfire Dr. Cummings gave us

some of the answers. If you don't already know, the dictionary will tell you that archaeology is the study of ancient ruins and peoples. From the things archaeologists dig up — the stones prehistoric man shaped into implements and utensils, the bones of the animals he killed, the ashes of his campfires, even the graves in which he buried his dead — these scientists attempt to recreate the life of long-vanished peoples, to make history of prehistory.

These pots and pans and tools and bones archaeologists call man's culture, his way of life. From them we learn about man's past — his heredity, the effects of his environment on his way of life, how his mind works, how he solved his problems, how and when he discovered or invented arts and industries, how civilization grew.

In other words, archaeology helps us understand the reasons back of the origin, growth, and fall of civilizations. Progress is based on trial and error. But, if we can learn from the lessons of prehistory and history, perhaps we can avoid making the mistakes of the past.

To accomplish this, however, we need every scrap of evidence we can get. Because no two peoples live in exactly the same way, cultures differing from group to group, from country to country, from century to century, archaeologists must dig all over the world. That was why our party was investigating the cliff dwellings of northern Arizona.

Dr. Cummings didn't keep us up too late. We were all tired after the hard day and soon began hunting for a warm place to spend the night, women at one end of the long cliff dwelling, men at the other. Louis and I chose one of the upper, windowless rooms in which to sleep, spreading one of our two blankets on the centuries-old floor of wind-blown dust and leaves and using the other as a cover. Almost within minutes stillness settled over the high-arched vault of the huge cave and its score of twentieth century intruders. Only the *chindi*, the spirits of the ancient cliff-dwellers, remained on guard. According to the Navaho Indians, these evil spirits, the ghosts of the dead, frequently appear at night in the form of men or birds or animals, bringing bad dreams and disease and even death to those who see them.

Now something had disturbed that silence. Wondering what had happened, Louis and I looked down the steeply sloping cave floor with its rows of terraced stone and mud houses and open courts or patios. Here and there on the lower roof-tops were other shadowy figures who, like us, had been roused from sleep by the scream. Following the direction of their gaze, we saw, to our left and a hundred feet below, a small campfire blazing redly in one of the open courts. The flickering light played over half a dozen figures huddled around a dark shape sprawled on the rock. Hushed voices and an occasional agonizing groan drifted up to us on the heels of the cool night breeze.

Our curiosity was high, but neither Louis nor I wanted to risk breaking an arm or leg by climbing down to the fire. After a few minutes the story was passed up from roof-top to roof-top, eventually reaching us.

One of the students, a young man we shall call Sam Jones, had elected to sleep alone in a second-story room. The room he picked had a side entrance, the sill of which could only be reached by a long step from the roof of an adjacent room, for directly below the doorway was a seven-foot drop to a small court. Jones had managed to scramble across from the neighboring roof and had gone to bed. Later in the night something had awakened him. Still half-asleep, he had opened his eyes and thought he saw one of the *chindi* in his room. Frightened, he had tried to back out through the narrow doorway but had gotten tangled in his blanket and had slipped and fallen, landing flat on his back on the stone platform below. According to the report that came to us, Jones claimed his back was broken.

There was nothing we could do to help and since the wind was growing colder, Louis and I went back to bed. But no one got much sleep the rest of the night. The first light of dawn found the entire party around the blazing campfire, drinking hot black coffee and eating breakfast from the meager supplies we had packed in.

Sam Jones still insisted his back was broken. There was only one thing to do — carry him out. We improvised a stretcher from a couple of stout poles and a pair of sweaters and, as soon as full daylight came, started back for the highway and our cars. There were only 8 younger men in the party and we took turns, four at a time, carrying the stretcher up and down the sand and rocks of Segie Canyon, to the accompaniment of a steady flow of groans from the injured man. Without even stopping to eat lunch, we made it back to the highway by four in the afternoon and loaded the still groaning Jones into Dr. Cummings' car.

The rest of us trailed along behind in the other cars. To add to our troubles it began to rain before we had gone more than a mile or two. Fighting rain and mud all the way, the last car in the procession, unfortunately the truck I was driving, didn't reach Kayenta until nearly midnight.

"But what happened," you ask, "to the injured Sam Jones?"

The doctor at the Indian hospital at Kayenta couldn't find anything wrong with him, but Jones still claimed his back was broken. So we drove him to a larger Indian hospital nearly a hundred miles away over even more primitive roads, getting stuck once or twice along the way. There we left him while the rest of us went back to our summer project of excavating Kinishba Pueblo in eastern Arizona. Sam showed up a week later. There had been nothing wrong with him but an attack of nerves. Too many *chindi!*

That was my introduction 30 years ago to the ancient *chindi* and Arizona cliff dwellings. Today's visitor shouldn't experience such hazards. There are better roads, some of them even being paved. Now you can drive almost to Betatakin's front door and find National Park Service rangers and naturalists there to guide you through the ruins.

But the prehistoric ruins haven't changed. A few more have been discovered, a few more excavated. An unknown number still lie buried beneath the desert sands or hidden away in remote canyons. Who the builders of these cliff dwellings were and what happened to them is the theme of our story.

# 2
# The
# First Indians

Christopher Columbus in 1492 wasn't the first to discover America. Even Leif Ericson and his Norsemen who landed on Greenland and the coast of New England five hundred years earlier were latecomers. Nearly 25,000 years ago Asiatic immigrants from Siberia crossed Bering Strait and discovered the New World.

How do we know this?

Because of the digging of archaeologists. Archaeologists agree that the ancestors of the American Indian came originally from Asia. Although American Indians range from short to tall, thin to fat, light brown to dark brown, long-heads to broad-heads, wavy-haired to straight-haired, snub-nosed to Roman-nosed (as on our Indian Penny), they look more like many of the inhabitants of Asia than they do anyone else.

Our story begins, then, some 25,000 years ago when the first Asiatic immigrants moved from Asia to North America. They didn't have to swim or use a boat. At Bering Strait the two continents are separated by little more than 50 miles of water. Back in the days of the Ice Age a great deal of northern North America and Asia was covered with massive ice sheets thousands of feet thick. With that amount of water frozen into ice, the sea level was lowered so much that these Asiatic immigrants probably walked across on dry land.

Once across in Alaska the newcomers made themselves at home. They were in a hunter's paradise. Millions of wild animals roamed the plains and forests of the New World. Here were such creatures as the mammoth, mastodon, camel, horse, bison, and ground sloth. None of these animals are living today. All of them became extinct at the close of the Ice Age. The horse, however, was later reintroduced by the first European explorers and colonists. But thousands of years ago many of these horses and other animals ended up roasting over a campfire. Even the climate was different then. With all that ice and snow around, it was cold and frequently wet.

Following the trail of these animals the immigrants wandered deeper and deeper into North America. Some moved down the eastern side of the Rocky Mountains into the high plains country. Others pushed down the west side of the mountains into the western United States.

Here and there groups stopped when they found country that suited them. Others continued on still further southward. Eventually their descendants spread out over all of the New World, even reaching the extreme southern tip of South America. When Columbus arrived on the scene, some eight to ten million Indians, descendants of these Asiatic immigrants, occupied North, Central and South America.

Not all of these early American Indians were alike in the

way they lived. Some were primarily big-game hunters
while others depended mainly for food on the seeds and
nuts and berries they could gather. The immigrants who
made their way down the east side of the Rocky Mountains
took advantage of the multitude of large game animals
roaming the grassy plains and became hunters. Those who
came down west of the Rockies seem to have been foragers,
living off wild vegetable foods and small game.

From Canada to Mexico archaeologists have discovered
scores of campsites of these first hunting Indians. Buried
with the ashes of their campfires and the discarded animal
bones are the lost or broken stone weapons with which they
killed these animals.

To most of us one flint spearhead looks just like another
flint spearhead. But not to an archaeologist. To him each
type is as distinctive as the different modern cars are to us.
Just as car models change from year to year, so styles of
spearheads changed from people to people, from century to
century.

Some of these early hunters liked thick and stubby spearheads. Some preferred long and slender ones. Others wanted
flutes or channels chipped in one or both sides. Not until
much later were spearheads notched like the familiar Indian
arrowheads. In fact, bows and arrows didn't enter the New
World from Asia until nearly the beginning of the Christian
Era.

These flint weapons, usually called projectile points by
the scientists, were used to tip spears or darts. Many early
peoples hurled their darts with an atlatl or spear thrower.
This was a piece of wood two or three feet long, with a
hand hold at one end and a socket at the other. The butt end

of the spear rested against the socket and the spear was balanced on top of the thrower, the added length of the thrower giving greater force to the hurled spear.

Each projectile point speaks its own language to the archaeologist, telling him what group of hunters made it and how long ago it was used. In many sites these stone projectile points are our only link with the past. Whatever implements and utensils of wood or fiber the people might have had have not survived the effects of weather and time.

There were many of these early hunting groups in the plains area — Sandia, Clovis, Folsom, Plainview, and a dozen others. Perhaps the most famous of these are the Clovis and Folsom, named after two sites in New Mexico where their remains have been found. Twelve thousand years ago Clovis hunters were killing mammoth and musk-ox and other giant animals with large grooved spearheads. Several thousand years later, toward the close of the Ice Age, Folsom men, their spears and darts tipped with small fluted points, hunted huge buffalo or bison from Montana to Texas.

At about this same time, west of the Rocky Mountains in the plateaus and deserts of Oregon, Nevada, Utah, and Arizona, other Indians were scratching for a living. Though these people hunted and ate nearly everything that walked or crawled or flew, they were primarily gatherers of wild plants. Instead of large projectile points, their characteristic utensils were baskets and nets and grinding stones. When they could find caves or rock shelters, they preferred to live in them rather than out in the open.

The end of the Ice Age brought death to most of the large animals roaming the plains. Mammoth, mastodon, giant bison, horse, camel, ground sloth, and saber-toothed tiger all vanished almost overnight. Scientists can't agree why it happened. It may have been due to overhunting or disease or famine or climatic change or a combination of these.

In any case, many of the big-game hunters, like their distant relatives west of the Rockies, were forced to turn to gathering. This was particularly true in the Southwest, that section of North America covering southwestern Colorado, southern Utah, southeastern Nevada, Arizona, New Mexico, extreme western Texas, and northern Sonora and Chihuahua in Mexico.

By 6000 B.C. a group of nomadic gatherers, called the Cochise people by archaeologists, were living in southeastern Arizona and southwestern New Mexico, collecting wild plant foods and hunting small game. By 3000 B.C., or shortly thereafter, these Cochise people began to grow corn, maize.

The art of farming was introduced into the Southwest from Mexico. Far to the south, in Mexico and Central America, other American Indians had, through long centuries of experimentation with wild grasses and other plants, discovered how to domesticate corn and beans and squash. Gradually these plants spread northward up the Sierra Madre Mountains, finally reaching the Cochise people inhabiting the mountain valleys along the present Arizona-New Mexico border.

Corn came first, followed a thousand or so years later by squash and then by beans. These were the trinity of food plants that usually went together to form the basic diet of most prehistoric southwesterners.

Shortly before the opening of the Christian Era the Cochise people learned how to make pottery from clay. This, too, came up from Mexico. With the addition of pottery to farming, the Cochise people began to settle down in more or less permanent villages of round pithouses. These houses were made by digging circular pits several feet deep in the ground and roofing them with poles, brush, and mud laid over a framework of upright poles. Archaeologists call this new culture the Mogollon, named after the Mogollon Mountains, which were in turn named for Don Juan Ignacio Flores de Mogollon, Captain General of New Mexico from 1712 to 1715.

Life in these small mountain valleys wasn't easy for the Mogollon people. During the next twelve to thirteen hundred years their arts and crafts remained comparatively simple.

Some of their implements and utensils, like corn-grinding stones, mortars and pestles, hoes, and grooved mauls, continued much as they had been. Others, like pottery, gradually improved, changing from plain red to red designs on a brown background, then to red decoration on white, and

Fig. 2. Mogollon pithouse at Bluff Ruin, Arizona.

— *Arizona State Museum*

finally to black designs on white. Tubular stone pipes were made for smoking tobacco, probably being used ceremonially. The bow and arrow were also introduced into the area and gradually replaced the spear and spear thrower.

For the most part Mogollon villages remained small, often being built on ridges or terraces above their valley farm lands. Houses were still pit structures, round to roughly rectangular in shape, generally with a long inclined entrance off to the east side. Some of the bigger villages also had one larger pithouse which may have served for ceremonial purposes.

They buried their dead in individual graves dug between the houses. Before a body was placed in one of these circular pits it was flexed, that is, the knees were drawn up toward the chin to make a tightly folded, compact bundle. Sometimes a pot or two was left as a burial offering. This shows that these people believed in some form of an afterworld. From a study of the skeletons archaeologists found that the Mogollon people were of medium height and body build, with broad and short heads.

As Mogollon population increased over the centuries, small bands split off and spread out along the mountains northward and westward. To the west, in the desert valleys of southern Arizona, they came in contact with another group of southwestern Indians. This was the Hohokam, so called from the Pima Indian term for the "ancient people."

The Hohokam seem to have been another branch of Cochise gatherers who chose to live in the desert rather than in the mountains. Like the Mogollon, they acquired agriculture — corn, squash, and beans, and later cotton — and pottery from Mexico, perhaps through trade with Mogollon peoples. Lacking adequate rainfall for their crops, they early began digging ditches or canals to bring water from the rivers to their distant fields. Within the next thousand years they developed an extensive irrigation system along the Salt and Gila Rivers. Many of these ancient canals are still in use today.

Like the Mogollon people, the Hohokam lived in square or rectangular houses of poles and mud built inside shallow pits. In later times, after 600 A.D., they imported a ceremonial ball game from Mexico and constructed huge ball courts up to two or three hundred feet in length, with earthen embankments along the sides. Still later, they obtained small copper bells from Mexico.

Unlike the Mogollon, they cremated their dead, depositing the ashes and burned bones in pits or trenches, later in pottery jars. For this reason archaeologists can't tell us what these Hohokam people looked like.

Also unlike the Mogollon, they developed into expert workers in both stone and shell. The presence of these shells indicates trade with peoples along the Gulf of California. Many of their ordinary implements and utensils were carefully made and frequently ornamented. They made comparatively little use of bone, in contrast to its considerable use in the Mogollon villages. But they manufactured more than their share of pottery vessels, decorating them with red designs on a buff background.

Further to the west and northwest of the Hohokam, along the Colorado River valley, lived still another early southwestern people. This was the Patayan, named after a Walapai Indian term signifying the "ancient ones." The Patayan may have sprung directly from some of the earlier desert-dwelling, food-collecting peoples or they may have arisen as a branch of the Hohokam.

These Indians, too, were farmers and potters. Their pottery was reddish-brown in color and occasionally was decorated with designs in red. Few remains of their houses have been found, and it is likely they lived in brush huts.

Up to this point we have been concerned with laying the foundation, the background, for prehistoric Indian life in the Southwest. A knowledge of all of these groups — Mogollon, Hohokam, and Patayan — is essential to an understanding of later developments.

But now it is time to turn our attention to the main subjects of our story — the Basketmakers and Cliff Dwellers of the Four Corners country.

# 3
# Baskets Before
# Houses and Pots

Our story begins in the Four Corners country, where Arizona, New Mexico, Colorado, and Utah come together at right angles. This is the only such place in the United States where four states meet.

This northern part of the Southwest includes much of the Colorado Plateau, a high tableland ranging from 5,000 to more than 10,000 feet above sea level. Radiating out from the Four Corners in all directions is a vast expanse of plateaus, terraces, buttes, mesas, cliffs, and canyons. Sagebrush and yucca and beargrass cover much of the lower country, with juniper and pinyon trees in the hills and pine and fir on the higher mountains.

To the geologist this is a fascinating region, for here are exposed North America's oldest and youngest rocks. To the scenic enthusiast it is a paradise. It includes the world-famed Painted Desert and the equally famous Petrified Forest. Here also are the Grand Canyon of the Colorado River, Meteor Crater, Sunset Crater, Monument Valley, Rainbow Bridge, and Glen Canyon Dam, one of the world's largest dams, creating a lake several hundred miles in length.

Fig. 3. Four Corners country, northern Arizona.

To the archaeologist this country is a gold mine. Literally thousands of prehistoric ruins dot the canyons and mesas. Some are large, some are small. Some have been excavated but most have not been touched. Though archaeologists have been exploring and digging in the Southwest for seventy-odd years, there are still untold numbers of ruins that have not yet even been discovered.

Here also you can see dozens of villages where modern descendants of these prehistoric American Indians are still living much as their ancestors did a thousand years ago.

For this is Indian country, a part of today's immense Hopi and Navaho Indian reservations. Here are no cities, no towns, no railroads, few paved highways. Only a handful of small Hopi Indian villages break the landscape, with here and there an occasional trading post or government building or cluster of Navaho hogans.

Two thousand years ago it wasn't even that crowded. Buzzards and jackrabbits and lizards had it pretty much to themselves.

Then a group of gatherers and small game hunters moved in. Who they were and where they came from we do not know. Perhaps they were desert dwellers from Utah and Nevada in search of better hunting and collecting grounds. Perhaps they were refugee Cochise people who split off from their relatives and migrated northward into cooler country. Then again, perhaps they had already been in the Four Corners area for some hundreds or thousands of years. If this was true, they certainly left no trace behind them to tell of their presence.

In any event, to this group of hunters and foragers corn and squash were introduced about the beginning of the Christian Era. Archaeologists aren't agreed where these people got their knowledge of farming. Some say it came from the east, from groups of Indian farmers along the Mississippi River who had shifted westward into the plains and mountains. Others argue that corn and squash were probably borrowed from some of the northern Mogollon peoples. This would seem to be the most logical explanation. Little more than 200 miles separated these northern settlers from the nearest Mogollon villages along the Arizona-New Mexico border.

For the next thousand years this Four Corners country was home to these first farmers. Archaeologists call them the Anasazi or "ancient ones"; they were so named by the Navaho Indians who settled among their ruined villages within the past three or four hundred years. Archaeologists divide Anasazi culture into two periods, an early Basketmaker and a later Pueblo or Cliff Dweller.

What these first Four Corners farmers called themselves, if anything, we do not know. Their discoverers coined the term Basketmaker because of the great number of baskets of all sizes and shapes they found in these early sites.

In most regions the archaeologist has to guess at the age of the pots and pans and people he digs up. But not in the Four Corners country. If he can find fragments of wood or even pieces of charcoal, the archaeologist is in business. For here he has a continuous calender covering the past 2,000 years. This is not the calendar with which we are all familiar but a calendar of tree rings.

Dendrochronology, as this science of tree rings is called, was the brainchild of an astronomer, Dr. A. E. Douglass of the University of Arizona. In attempting to extend sunspot records into the past, he turned to yellow pine trees near Flagstaff. Trees aren't ashamed of their great age. Each year, just beneath the bark, a tree grows a new ring, a wide ring in a rainy year, a narrow one in a dry year. By comparing and matching these characteristic patterns of thick and thin rings in living trees with those from timbers from historic and prehistoric Indian villages, Dr. Douglass was able to extend his calendar back to 59 B.C.

Now, whenever a piece of wood or charcoal is dug up in an ancient ruin, it can be dated by comparing its ring pattern with those on Douglass's master chart. In this way hundreds of archaeological sites in the Southwest have been given exact building dates.

Archaeologists had long known the Basketmakers were older than the people who built the massive stone-walled pueblos and cliff dwellings. Wherever the two had lived in the same place, Basketmaker remains were always found beneath those of the pueblo builders. Archaeologists had also discovered that there were two distinct Basketmaker periods. An early phase without pottery and with only a few signs of houses was followed by a later era with well-developed pottery and houses.

Now, with the advant of tree-ring dating, archaeologists were able to assign definite dates to each of these phases and also to the later pueblo periods. These are indicated in the following chart:

| PERIODS | TIME |
|---|---|
| Basketmaker (Sometimes called Basketmaker II) | 1–450 A.D. |
| Modified Basketmaker (Also called Basketmaker III or Post-Basketmaker) | 450–750 A.D. |
| Developmental Pueblo (Also called Pueblo I & II, or early Pueblo) | 750–1000 A.D. |
| Great Pueblo (Also called Pueblo III or Classic Pueblo) | 1000–1300 A.D. |
| Regressive Pueblo (Also called Pueblo IV) | 1300–1600 A.D. |
| Historic Pueblo (Also called Pueblo V) | 1600 to Present |

It should be emphasized that these dates are not exact. In 750 A.D., for example, the Basketmakers did not switch overnight into full-fledged Pueblo Indians. The change from one period to the next was usually gradual, often lasting half a century or more.

Sometimes the inhabitants of communuities were slow to

adopt new customs and new ideas. Even as today we often find backwoods villages within shooting distance of big cities, so it was in the prehistoric Southwest. Many people continued to live in pit houses long after their cousins were building great apartment houses of stone and mud.

In the sheer-walled canyons of the Four Corners country the Basketmakers found protection from the weather and soil and water for their corn and squash. This is a land of caves, caves, and more caves: Woodchuck Cave, White Dog Cave, Dupont Cave, Sunflower Cave, Obelisk Cave, Mummy Cave, Owl Head Cave, Red Rock Cave, Painted Cave, Step House Cave, Broken Flute Cave.

Many Basketmakers probably lived out in the open, perhaps in brush shelters of which, naturally enough, no trace remains today. But wherever caves were available, they moved in to take advantage of their shelter.

The word cave is actually a misnomer, making you think of a dark, deep cavern. Most Basketmaker caves are more like rock shelters, fairly shallow recesses near the bases of high sandstone cliffs. Some are small, but others are hundreds of feet in length and height.

It is because of these caves that we know as much as we do about the Basketmakers. Like most primitive people, Basketmaker women were not fussy housekeepers. They swept or tossed their rubbish into the nearest corner or down the slope in front of the rock shelter. The overhanging cave roof and the arid climate helped preserve implements and utensils that would normally rot away in a few years.

These early Basketmakers didn't do much remodeling of what Mother Nature had provided. Almost the only structures they built in caves were storage places for their crops.

Fig. 4. Broken Flute Cave in northern Arizona.

Fig. 5. Circular, slab-lined storage cist in Broken Flute Cave.

In the sandy floors they dug circular pits from three to five feet in diameter and from two to three feet in depth. Sometimes these cists were lined with thin sandstone slabs, the joints of which were chinked with bark, corn husks, or small rocks and then sealed with adobe mud. The floors were often covered with sandstone slabs or a bed of bark or grass or coated with mud. The larger cists were sometimes divided into bins by slab partitions set in the floor.

To keep out blowing sand and packrats and other burrowing animals most pits were provided with covers. The smaller pits were usually covered with round sandstone slabs set tightly in mud. The larger ones often had roofs of small poles and brush plastered with a layer of adobe mud.

Some of the largest cists, up to eight feet in diameter and four feet in depth, seem to have served as sleeping quarters. They were furnished with beds of grass, leaves, or shredded juniper bark and had pole and brush and mud roofs with a square hatchway in the center.

In some of these pits excavators have found stores of corn and seeds and gourds just as they were left there nearly 2,000 years ago. One such storage pit held over 700 ears of corn, all as perfectly preserved as if they had been packed away only a month or two before.

But more important to the archaeologist is that many of these storage pits were later used as burial cists. Fortunately for the archaeologist, the Basketmakers believed in a life after death and buried with the dead clothing and implements and utensils. Also fortunately for the archaeologist, the dryness of the caves mummified the bodies and preserved the materials buried with them.

Though we call these bodies mummies, they should not be confused with the Egyptian mummies you read about.

In prehistoric Egypt bodies were artificially embalmed and mummified. Here in the Southwest it was a natural process. Instead of decaying, the bodies just dried out, leaving the flesh, skin, nails, and hair much as they were in life.

In preparing a body for burial, it was flexed; that is, the knees were drawn up almost to the chin. The body was then wrapped in a rabbit-fur blanket or in a large woven bag split down one side. It was laid, generally on the side, in the storage cists and a large basket was often inverted over the face. With it were placed sandals, weapons, and ornaments. Finally the grave was covered with slabs of stone, poles, brush, and dirt. The survivors went on about their business, walking back and forth over the tombs of their relatives.

Multiple burials of two, three, and four bodies were common. One storage pit contained nineteen bodies jammed tightly together. This suggests that epidemics may sometimes have occurred. The mortality rate for infants and

Fig. 6. Flexed mummy from a cave site in northeastern Arizona.
— *Arizona State Museum*

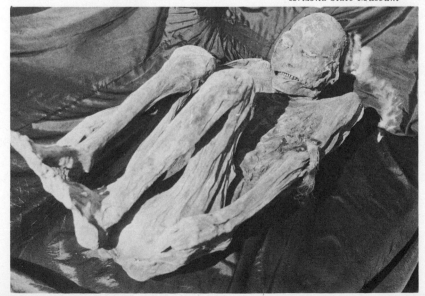

children was high. Babies were normally buried in their cradles while children were often placed in large baskets or woven bags.

Not all Basketmaker mummies dug up were human. Several dog burials have also been found. Two of these came from White Dog Cave, Arizona, one buried with a man, the other with a woman. The larger of the two dogs resembled a long-haired white collie, the smaller a shaggy-haired black and white terrier.

From a study of the human mummies, physical anthropologists tell us the Basketmaker people were Indians, much like many southwestern Indians of today. They were short, the men averaging a few inches above five feet tall, the woman a little less. They had long, rather narrow skulls, medium brown skins, and coarse straight black hair.

These burials and their accompanying offerings also tell us a great deal about Basketmaker arts and crafts, including clothing.

Except for sandals, the Basketmaker wardrobe of both men and women was limited. Although a few examples of what may have been "G-strings" or breechcloths have been found in caves, no mummy has ever been discovered wearing one. Women, however, often wore small aprons consisting of waist cords with attached fringes of strings of yucca fiber or cedar bark. The fringes on one such apron or skirt found on a female mummy contained more than a mile of yucca fiber string.

Since almost every burial was wrapped in a fur-cloth blanket, it is likely that these also served as robes for the living during cold weather and as blankets at night. These blankets were made by winding strips of rabbit fur around yucca cords and tying these together in closely spaced

Fig. 7. Basketmaker twined woven bags and shell jewelry.

parallel rows. Tanned deerskins were also fashioned into mantles or robes.

But the standard item in Basketmaker attire, for both the living and the dead, was a pair of sandals. You would readily understand why if you attempted to walk over this rough, rocky Four Corners country. These first sandals were square-toed, finely woven of yucca fiber cord and decorated with a toe fringe of buckskin, yucca fiber, or shredded juniper bark. They were fastened to the foot with cords passing through heel and toe loops and around the ankle.

The Basketmakers may have worn very little clothing, but they made up for that lack when it came to ornaments. To be well dressed meant having a bead necklace or two and perhaps a feather hair ornament. Beads are common in most Basketmaker sites. There are beads of carefully ground and polished stone, beads of olivella and abalone shell, beads of bone cut into short tubes, and beads of hard polished seeds.

The bright-colored feathers of such birds as bluebirds and woodpeckers were tied to bone or wooden pins to make hair ornaments or were tied in loops on strings and worn as pendants.

If there had been a beauty shop in the Four Corners country 2,000 years ago, its patrons would have been almost entirely men. At least this is the impression we get from a study of the hair styles of Basketmaker mummies. It seems that the men wore their hair long, carefully tied with cord in three bobs, a small one at each side of the head and a heavier one at the back. There are also several instances of queues, braided or wrapped with cord, hanging down the back.

In contrast to the elaborate hair-do of the men, that of the women was simple. Nearly every woman had her hair roughly hacked off to a length of two or three inches.

We don't have to look far to find an explanation for this practice. A great deal of human hair was used as a fiber in weaving bags and nets and aprons and in making strong cords. It was probably much easier for a woman to chop off a chunk of her own hair when she ran out of weaving material than it was for her to attempt to clip a lock from her husband's head.

Human hair cord is one of the characteristic features of Basketmaker culture. Archaeologists have even found caches in caves where hanks of human hair were stored away for a rainy day. Dog hair was also frequently used for cordage.

But the most common fibers for making string and cord were yucca and Indian hemp, the latter forming extremely fine, even strands. These fibers were used to make sandals, aprons, snares, nets, bags, and carrying bands.

One rabbit net from White Dog Cave in northern Arizona is one of the largest pieces of prehistoric textiles ever found in North America. When it was unrolled, it proved to be 3 feet 8 inches wide and 240 feet long. It contained nearly 20,000 feet of two-ply Indian hemp, with another 500-odd feet of heavier yucca cord binding the sides and edges. In two small sections of the net human hair had been woven in with the Indian hemp. Such nets were used in community hunts, probably being set up across the mouth of a canyon, blocking the exit. Hunters would then come down the canyon, beating the bushes and making a racket to drive rabbits or other small game into the nets where they could be captured.

Twined woven bags were also characteristic of Basketmaker culture. These were flexible sacks, roughly egg-shaped and ranging from 1½ inches to 2 feet or more in length. They were woven of two-ply Indian hemp string and decorated with woven or painted designs in black and red on the natural yellow-brown background of the Indian hemp. These bags were used by Basketmaker men, women, and children for everything from jewelry or medicine sacks to burial coffins.

But the one feature of the Basketmaker people that gave

them their name was the manufacture of baskets — bowls, shallow trays, trinket baskets, globular jars, carrying baskets, water bottles.

Lacking pottery, they had to use baskets as their pots and pans and storage boxes. And they made them by the hundreds.

Most baskets were built up from the base by the coiling process. Each coil, consisting of two small willow rods laid side by side and topped by a yucca fiber padding, was sewed to the one below with a thin willow splint. Women basketmakers used a bone awl to punch the holes through which the sewing splints were inserted.

Some baskets were so tightly and closely woven that they were waterproof. The Indians could have used these baskets to cook stews and other semiliquid foods by dropping in hot rocks until the liquid boiled.

Fig. 8. Basketmaker-type coiled baskets from Arizona.

*— Arizona State Museum*

Many baskets were ornamented with designs in black or, occasionally, in both black and red. These colored designs were made by dyeing the wooden sewing splints.

Shallow trays were the most common forms, ranging from a few inches up to two feet and more in diameter. They were probably used for serving food, for winnowing seeds, and perhaps in certain games.

Carrying baskets, as the name implies, were used for carrying loads on the back. The largest of the coiled baskets, they often measured 30 inches in diameter at the top by 20 inches deep, tapering to a point at the bottom. All had pairs of loops, generally of human hair string, fastened to their sides for the attachment of woven headbands. Carrying baskets were also commonly used as coverings for burials, perhaps the bodies of their former owners.

Since few caves had running water, it had to be carried up from the nearest stream or spring or down from natural rain-water basins on the mesa tops. Water jars were, therefore, of major importance. These were shaped somewhat like the carrying baskets but had smaller openings to prevent water from splashing out. Some even seem to have had string-hinged covers. The inner surfaces of these baskets were coated with pinyon gum to make them watertight. Like carrying baskets, they were provided with human hair string loops for carrying bands.

These earliest Basketmakers were farmers, raising corn and squash in the flat canyon bottoms. Just how good farmers they were we do not know as no traces of their fields remain. Shelled corn found stored in baskets and skin bags perhaps indicates seed carefully selected and stored away for the next year's planting. We do know their agricultural tools were limited, consisting only of digging sticks to loosen up the ground. These were hardwood sticks from 3 to 3½ feet in length, with one end smoothed to form a thin blade or a flat point.

However, like most beginning farmers, the Basketmakers couldn't raise enough food to last them through the year. Women still had to spend much of their time harvesting the wild fruits and seeds growing in the valleys and making occasional trips into the mountains to collect pinyon nuts and acorns. This is proved by the stores of grass seeds, sunflower seeds, chokecherries, pinyon nuts, and acorns uncovered in storage cists in caves.

Nor were the men idle. To add meat to their scanty rations, they hunted and trapped birds and animals. This is shown by the quantity of bird and animal bones littering most cave sites. To capture such small game as birds, rabbits, gophers, badgers, and field mice, they set slip-noose snares and nets similar to the one we described from White Dog Cave. For larger animals, deer, mountain sheep, and bears, the hunters used spears hurled with the atlatl or spear thrower.

To survive in such a harsh land, the early Basketmakers had to work, and work hard. But they found time now and then to relax. Deer hoof rattles, bone whistles, ceremonial wands, bundles of feathers, and medicine bags all seem to indicate religious ceremonies and ceremonial dances. Gaming sticks, gaming bones, and stone and bone dice lead archaeologists to believe the Basketmakers were not above playing games of chance.

Some of them were also artists. Numbers of painted pictures have been found on the smooth rock walls of caves and cliffs. These usually show square-shouldered human figures and hand prints in red, white, or yellow paint. These

Fig. 9. Petroglyphs or rock carvings made by the prehistoric Anasazi of northeastern Arizona.

Fig. 10. Pueblo-like rock carvings or petroglyphs from north-western Arizona.

paintings, called pictographs by the archaeologist, were not writing. Some of them may have had some religious or ceremonial meaning, but many of them were probably drawn just for the fun of it.

Incomplete as our story is, this was early Basketmaker life as it was in the Four Corners country nearly 2,000 years ago.

# 4
# The Basketmakers
# Settle Down

Along about 450 or 500 A.D. the Basketmakers of the Four Corners country began to settle down in permanent houses grouped in small villages.

This revolution in living marks the beginning of what archaeologists call the Basketmaker III Period or Late Basketmaker or Post-Basketmaker or Modified Basketmaker. To avoid confusion, we shall continue to call these people Basketmakers, using the prefixes early and late only by way of emphasis.

We should remember that the change from early to late Basketmakers didn't take place at the same time in all parts of the Four Corners country. New ideas and new inventions spread slowly 2,000 years ago. Also, some groups were conservative, reluctant to accept new fangled contraptions they didn't know anything about. We should also remember that, though the way of life changed, the people themselves didn't change a bit. The later Basketmakers were merely the grandsons and great-grandsons of the earlier Basketmakers.

But before we tell you how the Basketmakers learned to

build houses, we shall have to retrace our steps a few hundred years. In the last chapter we said the Basketmakers erected no permanent structures except storage pits. This is true for more than 90 per cent of the Four Corners country, but it is not true for one small section of the Animas Valley in southwestern Colorado.

There, archaeologists have excavated a couple of early Basketmaker villages. The rings of charred timbers show us that they were occupied from about 46 A.D. to 330 A.D. Some of these first houses were built in a rock shelter, others on a man-made sloping terrace. Nearly fifty individual houses were located in the two places, but only a few were thought to have been lived in at the same time.

The houses were roughly circular to oval in outline, from 8 to 30 feet in diameter, with slightly sunken, saucer-shaped floors. The walls were constructed of wooden sticks and small timbers laid horizontally in mud, with domed roofs of logs and brush and mud. Sunken in the clay floor of each house were from two to six slab-lined or jug-shaped storage cists. In addition, some houses had beehive-shaped mud cists built above the floor level.

There was no doubt about these being Basketmaker houses built by Basketmaker peoples. In and around the houses and storage pits, or laid away with the eighty-one burials dug up, were most of the typical Basketmaker implements and utensils and ornaments we read about in the preceding chapter.

This unusual discovery has so far not been duplicated elsewhere. All we can say is that the idea of house building didn't take hold with the rest of the early Basketmakers. Perhaps it represented too much work. Or perhaps the others didn't want to feel tied down to any one place.

Fig. 11. Segie Canyon, northern Arizona, in the heart of Basketmaker country.

Fig. 12. Basketmaker pithouse in Broken Flute Cave.
*— Arizona State Museum*

In any event, for most of the Basketmakers house construction did not make its appearance until somewhere around 500 A.D. When the idea did arrive, possibly from the Mogollon region, no standard building code came with it. Although practically all late Basketmaker houses were pithouses, Basketmaker architects seem to have had their own ideas about how these should be built.

As a result house plans frequently varied from village to village and from area to area in size and shape and interior arrangements. Some of the earliest were circular in form while others were oval. Later houses tended more toward a rectangular or square contour with rounded corners. Diameters ranged from 9 feet to 20 to 25 feet, with floor levels from 2 to 4 or 5 feet below the surface of the ground. The interior walls might be plastered with clay but more commonly they were lined with flat stone slabs. Sometimes a few rows of adobe bricks were laid on top of the slabs. Sometimes poles or reeds coated with clay formed the side walls.

Many pithouses had a southern vestibule or antechamber separated from the main part of the house by a low ridge of clay or a low partition wall of stone slabs. Some even consisted of two rooms, a huge main room and a smaller vestibule, with a short tunnel connecting the two. Others omitted the vestibule but had low clay ridges extending from a central fireplace to the southern corners of the room. Still others had a low bench running around the inside of the house.

Although some of the smaller circular pit houses had more or less conical or domed roofs of poles and brush plastered with clay, most pithouses had flat-topped superstructures. Four forked-top posts of juniper, pine, or fir, set in the floor, supported a rectangular framework of heavy horizontal logs. On this frame were laid parallel timbers from 2 to 3 inches apart. Smaller poles, their ends placed in the ground outside the pit or at the back of the bench, were leaned against the platform. The entire structure was then covered with brush and twigs and coated with a layer of mud or clay.

Houses with vestibules were entered through side or roof entrances opening into the antechamber. Most of the later houses without antechambers seem to have been entered by ladders through the smoke-hole hatchway in the center of the roof. Simple posts with projecting branch stubs or with cut-out steps may have been the first form of ladders. But true ladders have been found in some of the earliest houses. These were made by lashing cross-rungs to two parallel poles with split willow or yucca cords.

Floors were usually smoothed and plastered with clay,

Fig. 13. Basketmaker-type pithouse at Forestdale, Arizona.
— *Arizona State Museum*

but occasionally they were paved with flat stone slabs. Near the middle of the room was the central cooking and heating system. This was a round, sometimes rectangular, fire pit lined with hard-baked clay or stone and frequently encircled with a raised plaster rim. Immediately overhead was an open hatchway serving, in many cases, as both smoke hole and doorway.

Such partly underground, thick-walled houses would have been warm in winter and relatively cool in summer. But the Basketmakers also invented an efficient air-conditioning system. In a house with a vestibule and side entrance, the heat rising from the fire and passing out through the hatchway would draw cool air in through the vestibule. Later, when the antechamber and side entrance were abandoned, a ventilating shaft was dug down at one side of the house. From the bottom a short horizontal shaft led into the house at floor level. To prevent this draft of air from blowing directly against the fire, a deflector, generally a slab of stone, was set in the floor between the ventilator wall opening and the firepit.

Since the ventilating shaft had once been the actual house entrance, there was probably some ceremonial significance attached to it and to the deflector. As we shall see, these features were later incorporated in their ceremonial structures.

Another ceremonial feature found in many Basketmaker pithouses was a small hole filled with clean sand. This oval or round hole was generally located on the opposite side of the firepit from the deflector stone. Archaeologists believe that this represents the so-called sipapu found in the floors of later-day ceremonial houses. To the modern Pueblo Indians the sipapu symbolized the mythical point of emergence through which their ancestors made their way from the underworld to the surface of the earth. Archaeologists conjecture that, in the days before community ceremonial houses were built, each dwelling may have had its own shrine.

There was little or no furniture in these houses. By the time a family moved in its ordinary housekeeping necessities — a grinding stone or two, a mortar and pestle, a few cooking pots, food bowls, and water jars, some carrying baskets and storage bags hanging from the rafters alongside a baby cradle, together with assorted digging sticks and weapons and sleeping blankets — there wasn't much room for anything else. Some dwellings had small storage recesses in the wall, perhaps for jewelry baskets or rodent-skin sacks full of odds and ends. Some also had occasional small to medium-sized holes in the floor which may have served as storage places.

Even though the Basketmakers now had permanent houses where they could store various and sundry items, they continued to build storage pits. These were usually slab-lined, from 2 to 8 feet in diameter and from 2 to 3 feet in depth. They were covered with a conical or domelike roof of poles, brush, and clay. Some storage bins were also built entirely above ground. These pits and bins were probably used for the storage of corn and other foods. In one pithouse village in western New Mexico there were forty-eight of these storage pits.

Basketmaker houses were irregularly grouped in small clusters to form villages. These were usually small, consisting of from half a dozen up to fifteen or twenty individual dwellings. Toward the close of the period, along in the 700's, villages were frequently much larger in size. One or two have been reported as having had nearly a hundred pithouse structures.

Although many villages were built out in the open, generally on ridges where water wouldn't drain into the houses, the Basketmakers didn't give up cave life. They knew a good thing when they found it. Obelisk Cave, Broken Flute Cave, Vandal Cave, Ram's Horn Cave, Step House Cave, Pocket Cave, and numerous others continued to be occupied. In each cave archaeologists have found the remains of one or two or more pithouses and their associated slab-lined storage pits. Due to the lack of suitable living space, most pithouse villages in caves were small.

In fact, late Basketmaker house construction may have had its beginnings in such cave sites as Obelisk and Vandal. The occupation of Obelisk Cave, for example, was dated by tree rings to the latter part of the fifth century, 470-89 A.D.

However, we should mention that many archaelogists view these dates with some suspicion. As they point out, in nearby Broken Flute Cave and half a dozen other caves the building of similar pithouses by similar people using similar implements and utensils did not take place until 620 A.D. or later. Perhaps the Obelisk Cave inhabitants used old timbers that had been left there by earlier peoples. That would explain the difference in dates. But just what the correct answer is we can't say at present.

As we have seen, the Basketmakers were ceremonially inclined. During the eighth century, possibly a little earlier, they seem to have begun adding a separate religious or ceremonial structure to some of their villages. These were much larger than the average-sized dwelling, large enough in most cases, perhaps, for the entire village population to participate in ceremonial dances or celebrations. They were, however, built after the same general pattern as the ordinary pithouse.

One of these large ceremonial pithouses was uncovered in Chaco Canyon, New Mexico, at a site called by the Navaho Indians Shabik'eshchee Village, "Sun Picture Place." This structure was circular in shape and measured about 3 feet in depth and 36 feet in diameter inside the 2-foot-wide bench that circled the wall. The inner walls, both above and below the bench, were faced with flat stone slabs. The top of the bench itself was coated with adobe plaster. As in many of the houses, there was a deflector stone set in the floor between the rectangular firepit and the remains of a ventilator opening in the wall. Since the latter was too small to have served as a doorway, entrance was probably made through a hatchway in the flat-topped roof.

An even earlier example of what may have been a ceremonial structure was excavated in Broken Flute Cave. This consisted of a roughly circular area over 30 feet in diameter ringed by a single row of sandstone slabs set on edge.

From what we have seen, it is evident that there was no rigid custom covering methods of building in the entire Four Corners country. From Durango and Mesa Verde in Colorado westward into Utah, southward into northern Arizona's cliffs and canyons, and back eastward into New Mexico each area developed its own local standards. The picture we have presented is a composite one. It is not typical of any one area but shows some features found in each major region.

As century followed century, these differences, both in architecture and in arts and crafts, tended to widen. Yet there is always present a basic Anasazi pattern that runs through every phase of life.

# 5
# Pots and Other Borrowed Odds and Ends

These late Basketmakers were great borrowers. Another important household item they acquired from the Mogollon area to the south was pottery. The Mogollon people had been making and using pottery since about the beginning of the Christian Era. By 300 A.D., a date confirmed by tree rings, it had spread northward to the Bluff site, a Mogollon village in the Forestdale Valley of east central Arizona.

But the Basketmakers seem to have struggled along without pots and pans for several hundred years longer before the invention finally reached them. When they did find out about pottery, they got the idea before they did the knowledge of how to make it.

Archaeologists think this because they have found numerous fragments of thick-walled mud dishes in the refuse heaps of many Basketmaker cave villages. These crude vessels were not true pottery as they had not been fired. Yet they had been deliberately shaped into shallow, traylike bowls. To prevent them from cracking while drying, shredded juniper bark and other fibrous materials had been mixed with the dark adobe mud.

Fig. 14. Basketmaker unfired fiber-tempered mud bowl.

Some of the vessels had been built up of thick coils or ropes of clay, but many had been molded in baskets. This is indicated by the clear imprints of the basket weaves on the outsides of the bowls.

They look like crude imitations, copies, of true pottery, as if their makers had heard about pots but had never seen them. Perhaps some Basketmaker men, off on a trading expedition to one of the Mogollon villages, saw women making clay jars. When the traders returned home, they told their wives about these new utensils that could be put directly in the fire. When the Basketmaker women tried the process, these crude mud vessels may have been the result.

What they were used for we do not know. They were useless as either water jars or cooking pots, although they could have been used as containers for dry food. They must have served some purpose as the Basketmakers continued to make them long after they had learned how to manufacture real pottery.

If the date for the Basketmaker house in Obelisk Cave is correct, true pottery made its appearance in the Four Corners country during the latter part of the fifth century. If it is not, we have to add another hundred years to that figure.

Although Basketmaker pottery probably owes its origin to the Mogollon area, it was not a chip off the old block. Most Basketmaker pottery was gray or grayish-white in

Fig. 15. Plain gray Basketmaker jar from northeastern Arizona.

Fig. 16. Black-on-white Basketmaker bowls from northeastern Arizona.

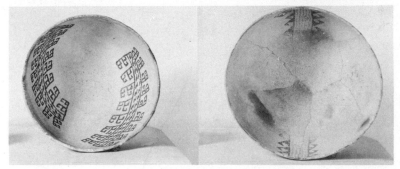

color, not red or reddish-brown like Mogollon vessels. When designs were painted on the inner surface of bowls, they were black not red.

Most Basketmaker pottery designs were simple, much like the band and panel designs on their basketry. The black paint was probably made by boiling the juice of such plants as bee weed. This was put on the vessels with a brush made by chewing the end of a yucca leaf until the fibers softened. Almost from the very beginning of pottery making, archaeologists can recognize differences in styles of decoration between various sections of the Four Corners country.

But most of the pottery the Basketmakers made was undecorated, plain gray in color. Sometimes the surfaces were smoothed and polished but more often they were rough and rather uneven. Jars of half a dozen shapes and sizes were the most common forms, along with pitchers, ladles, and a few bowls. Many jars had perforated clay lugs on the sides for easier carrying.

These locally made gray and black-on-white pots were not the only ones used by the Basketmakers. They seem to have had a fancy for the pottery manufactured by their neighbors to the south. At least numbers of these red and brown and decorated Mogollon bowls and jars have been found in many Basketmaker villages.

With the addition of pots and pans to Basketmaker household utensils, the standard of living went up. Food could now be cooked in a greater variety of ways directly over the fire. Soups and stews could be made with less time and effort and other dishes were added to the menu. Water and other materials could be better transported in jars of pottery. Pottery jars also made better rat-proof storage vessels than baskets. Round clay jar stoppers were even used to seal storage and water jars.

This doesn't mean the Basketmakers stopped making baskets and bags. They continued to manufacture them in considerable quantity, much the same kinds as they had in the earlier period. They still used baskets for storage, as shown by the fourteen baskets of corn, beans, and seeds uncovered in one cave pithouse.

They still made bands or tumplines for carrying baskets on their backs. These were of woven yucca cord, often with painted designs, or of two or three yucca leaves sewed together, with loops at either end.

Other household furnishings included woven mats of juniper bark, yucca fiber, or grass, wooden firedrills and hearths for starting fires, grass brooms, and pot rests. The last were circular doughnut-shaped rings of yucca leaves or juniper bark in which round-bottomed pots could be set.

Fig. 17. Basketmaker woven fiber bag from northeastern Arizona.

Fig. 18. Basketmaker carrying-bands of yucca cord and yucca leaves.

Since modern Pueblo Indian women carry their water jars on similar yucca fiber rings on top of their heads, it is likely that ancient Basketmaker women followed the same practice in transporting water from the springs and streams up to the caves. Small branches bent double served as tongs and pieces of hollowed wood as spoons.

The standard of living went up another notch when beans were borrowed from the Mogollon people. This was an important addition because beans furnished proteins to supplement the carbohydrate diet of corn and squash. New and somewhat larger varieties of corn were also introduced about this same time. Planting and tilling of the soil was still done with the wooden digging stick.

Even though the Basketmakers now had three dependable food crops in corn, squash, and beans, they kept on collecting pinyon nuts, grass seeds, roots, and other wild vegetable products. These added variety to their diet. Some of these plants, however, may have been gathered for medicinal purposes.

The Basketmakers continued to grab what was offered them in trade by the Mogollon and other neighboring peoples. In this way they acquired the stone ax, the grooved maul or hammer, and the bow and arrow.

The bow and arrow proved to be superior to the spear thrower or atlatl. They had far greater accuracy and range and were more efficient in the killing of birds and small animals. It wasn't long before the old gave way to the new and the bow and arrow took the spear thrower's place as the major weapon.

The Basketmaker bow was simply made of a single piece of tough wood about three feet long, grooved at both ends for the sinew bowstring.

Fig. 19. Fragments of Basketmaker bows and arrows.

Basketmaker arrows were usually compound, made up of a main shaft of cane and a foreshaft of hard wood. The cane shafts were bound at intervals with sinew to prevent them from splitting. There were a number of types of foreshafts, each adapted for a different purpose. Some were notched to hold small arrowheads, others were sharpened to points, and still others had large blunt ends to stun birds and other small game.

For hundreds of years the Basketmakers had been chipping flint, chalcedony, jasper, petrified wood, and quartzite into spearheads and knife blades and drills. It wasn't any trick for them to cut down the size of their spearheads and make smaller, notched points to fit their arrows. They still manufactured larger points and blades which they lashed in the split or notched ends of short or long pieces of wood and used as knives and spears.

Two other newly borrowed stone implements which aided the Basketmakers in house construction and other odd jobs were grooved mauls or hammers and axes.

Before the Indians acquired stone axes, it is thought that they felled big trees by means of fire. But with sharp stone axes they could chop trees down more quickly and easily. Grooved mauls or hammers would have been equally useful in breaking up sandstone slabs or in driving posts. These mauls were hafted to a wooden handle by wrapping a pliable stick around the groove and tying it with yucca cord. In the specimen illustrated in this chapter the wooden stick around the groove has been broken.

Late Basketmaker men and women seem not to have worn any more clothing than their ancestors did. But what they did wear was much more elaborately made and decorated.

— *Arizona State Museum*

Fig. 20. Basketmaker chipped stone drills, arrowheads, spearheads and knifeblades.

Fig. 21. Basketmaker grooved stone mauls.

— *Arizona State Museum*

As we would expect, women set the fashion. Small aprons were still their one and only garment. Some of them were still made of strings of yucca fiber or of shredded juniper bark suspended from a waist cord. But many were now woven of fine yucca or other cord to form a panel measuring 2 to 3 inches wide by 5 to 6 inches long. These had both woven and painted designs in black, red, yellow, pink, blue, and brown. From the bottoms of these woven panels the warp threads hung down to form a heavy fringe.

Men's attire, on the other hand, without exception seems to have been limited to footwear. If they ever wore loincloths, few, if any, have been found in their houses or laid away in graves with their bodies. The one possible exception is represented by the more than half dozen long narrow sashes braided of white and brown dog hair. These were discovered in two late Basketmaker cave villages in northeastern Arizona. It seems probable that they were made to be worn around the waist, but we do not know whether they were worn as clothing or as ceremonial attire.

The standard item of Basketmaker wearing apparel, for men, women, and children, continued to be a pair of sandals. But the earlier fringed, square-toed type had gone out of style. It was replaced by a scallop-toed sandal, finely made and decorated in color. These were woven of Indian hemp or fine yucca cord. Most were decorated with either woven designs in red, yellow, and black on the upper surfaces or raised designs on the soles. Many sandals had both types of decoration.

We wonder why the makers of these sandals should have spent so much time and effort in producing decorations that would be hidden by the wearer's foot or by the ground below. It may have been vanity, but perhaps a more likely answer lies in the fact that these people were craftsmen, driven by a desire to beautify everything they possibly could. There was, however, a practical value to the raised decoration on the sole. It both thickened the sandal and formed an effective tread for walking on rough or slippery surfaces.

Although the scallop-toed sandal was by far the most common type, the Basketmakers also made half a dozen other varieties. The next most abundant sandal was round-toed, also finely woven, and also often with a raised design on the bottom. In addition, there were a few round- and square-toed sandals plaited or woven of yucca fiber or crushed yucca leaves. These were not decorated.

It looks as if the plaited sandals may have been used as overshoes in cold or wet weather. They were larger than

Fig. 22. Late Basketmaker scallop-toed sandals.

— *Arizona State Museum*

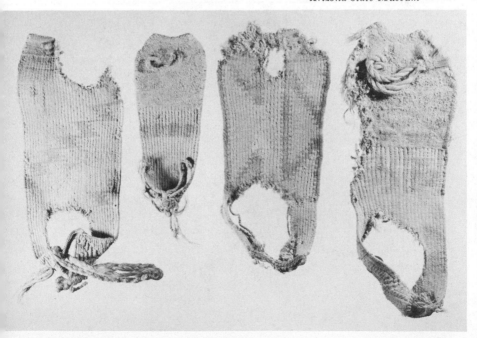

normal, were frequently padded on the inside with corn husks or juniper bark, and the soles were often found coated with mud.

Sandals were attached to the foot by one of two methods. The most common style was similar to that used in the earlier period, with a cord passing through heel and toe loops and around the ankle. The second device consisted of a series of loops on each side of the sandal which were connected with cord across the top of the foot.

Just like today's shoes, Basketmaker sandals didn't last forever. In time the soles wore through, generally either at the heel or near the toe, and the sandals were thrown away. Hundreds of such worn-out sandals have been dug up in cave sites. But 1500 years ago there were thrifty individuals who tried to repair their favorite footgear. Several have been found with patches cut from other sandals and sewn over holes. One even had a piece of rawhide fastened with rawhide strips over a hole near the toe end.

For winter wear rabbit-fur blankets continued to be manufactured, but, like square-toed sandals, they were rapidly going out of fashion. Taking their place were softer and lighter robes of turkey feathers. These were made by splitting the turkey quill and wrapping the feathers spirally around heavy yucca cords. Small downy feathers were also used for even softer lighter blankets.

So many turkey feathers were used to make robes and for other purposes that some archaeologists believe the Basketmakers domesticated the turkey. At least turkey pens or enclosures have been found in a number of Basketmaker cave villages. But other archaeologists think the Basketmakers only kept turkeys captive and that it was the later Pueblo Indians who actually domesticated our favorite Thanksgiv-

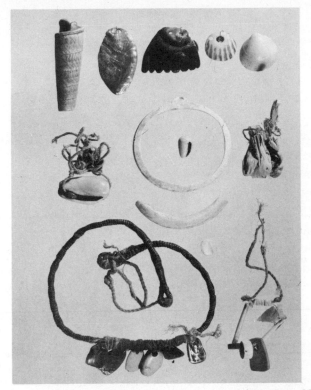

— *Arizona State Museum*

Fig. 23. Late Basketmaker shell ornaments.

ing bird. Since there has been a lack of turkey bones in most Basketmaker village refuse heaps the fowls seem not to have been eaten but to have been kept only for their feathers.

We don't know as much about late Basketmaker styles of hair-do as we did about those of their predecessors. Both men and women seem to have worn their hair in long braids. Human hair was still twisted and braided into string, but it seems to have been cut off the heads of both sexes, not just of the women. Several mummies of men have been found with their hair clipped to a length of three or four inches.

Like their ancestors, the Basketmakers were addicted to

the wearing of ornaments — feather hair ornaments, beads, necklaces, pendants, and bracelets.

Shell jewelry was common. The presence of abalone shells from the Pacific Coast and glycymeris, olivella, and other shells from the Gulf of California indicate how widely the Basketmakers traded. This doesn't mean the Basketmakers hiked all the way to the coast or to the gulf to trade for them. Probably they got the shells from neighboring groups who were closer to the sources of supply, like the Patayan, Hohokam, or Mogollon peoples. Judging by the amount of shell found in most Basketmaker sites, trade in this commodity must have been heavy.

Under a rock in a cave in northern Arizona archaeologists uncovered 1720 olivella shells strung on a cord 42 feet long. In another cave in Canyon del Muerto (Canyon of Death), excavators came across the mummy of an old woman that had been buried under the cave floor in late Basketmaker times. Several centuries later Pueblo Indians, in laying a slab floor just above the burial, had torn off the legs of the mummy and thrown them down beside the body. Probably at the same time they had looted whatever baskets and other offerings were in sight. Even a thousand years ago there were Indians who collected antiques and were not above grave robbing when the chance came. But in this case they seem to have been in too big a hurry to grab what they could and run. For they missed a unique ornament. Under the feather blanket, encircling the left wrist of the old woman, archaeologists found an armlet of 200 olivella shells strung on yucca cord, with a beautiful set of turquoise in the center.

Turquoise was another late Basketmaker acquisition. This bright blue stone quickly became popular, until today it is the favorite gem of most southwestern Indians. Veins of turquoise occur throughout the Southwest and many of these were mined in prehistoric times by the Pueblo Indians. We do not know whether the Basketmakers mined their own or whether they secured it by trade from other Indian groups.

Turquoise was cut and shaped into beads and pendants and was also used in inlays or mosaics. These were made by covering pieces of wood or basketry with chips of turquoise and shell set in pitch.

The Basketmakers didn't spend all their waking hours working. They seem to have had an elaborate ceremonial and religious life. This is indicated not only by the religious structures and ceremonial features we saw in the dwellings but also by the host of probable ceremonial objects uncovered in most Basketmaker villages. These range from small medicine bags to bone and stone dice sets, prayer sticks with feathers tied to them, corncobs with sticks or feathers inserted in one or both ends, bundles of feathers, lumps of mineral pigment, and smooth stone disks.

There are also a number of other items which may have had ceremonial significance. One of these is the so-called tobacco pipe. These small tapered cylinders were made of stone or clay, hollowed at one end and drilled at the other. Several have wooden or bone pipe bits secured in the mouth end with pitch. They look more like cigar holders than they do pipes. In some of these the Indians seem to have smoked tobacco, possibly wild tobacco, in others similar dried plants. It is probable that smoking was a ritual connected with certain ceremonies. We don't know too much about the kind of tobacco smoked in these pipes. Tobacco seems to have spread northward from Mexico

Fig. 24. Basketmaker medicine bag with dice sets, lumps of kaolin, and stone discs.

Fig. 25. Basketmaker stone and clay pipes.

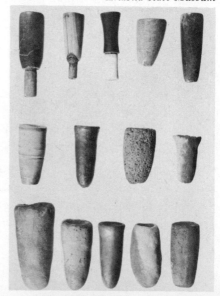

along with corn and other food plants. In some areas it was cultivated, in others gathered wild. Generally it was mixed with certain plants before it was smoked.

Two other articles made of clay, human figurines and funnel-shaped objects, were also presumably associated with some ritual. The figurines were crude models of human figures, generally females, oval to rectangular in shape, and from 1 to 4 inches long. The other clay objects were somewhat smaller, shaped like Basketmaker carrying baskets and decorated with punched geometric designs. Just what they could have been used for we do not know.

The Basketmakers also began playing their first real musical instrument, the flute. A number of carefully made, six-hole flutes have been dug up in cave sites. They were hollowed out of long elder branches and bound with sinew to prevent cracking. Two even were ornamented with bird

Fig. 26. Pair of Basketmaker flutes found under a pithouse floor in Broken Flute Cave.

*— Arizona State Museum*

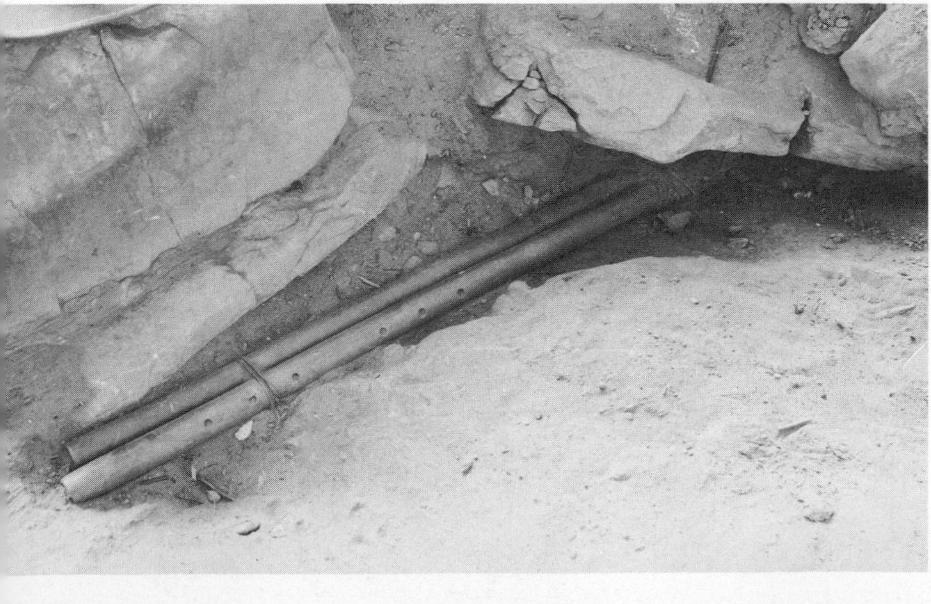

feathers. Like the tobacco pipes, these flutes were probably used only in certain ceremonies.

Aside from the implements and utensils found in their houses, much of our information about these late Basket-makers comes from their burials.

Most burials were now single rather than multiple as in the preceding period. Even though the people lived in villages, there were no definite cemeteries. Some bodies were laid away in abandoned storage cists, but more often they were tucked in crevices between rocks or in shallow pits scattered throughout the villages.

The graves were frequently lined with strips of juniper bark, with a covering of the same material above the body. Bodies were still flexed and were still wrapped in fur or feather blankets. Baskets, bags, and sandals were the chief burial offerings, along with numerous other objects such as food, clothing, and ornaments.

A description of the features and contents of many of these graves would be informative, but we shall only tell you about one of the most unusual. This was what has been called "The Burial of the Hands," discovered in the Canyon of Death in the same cave in which archaeologists found the mummy with the handsome olivella shell armlet.

Digging into a storage cist, the excavators came upon two hands, palms up, and their attached forearms lying on a bed of grass. The elbow bones were touching the slab sides of the cist, indicating that the rest of the body had never been put in with the hands and arms. Besides one arm were two pairs of finely woven sandals decorated in black and red. Near the other arm was a small basket almost half full of white shell beads. On the wrists were three elaborate shell necklaces. A large basket covered the hands and arms and their offerings.

What mystery lies behind this strange burial we shall never know. The secret is buried with the hands.

We have brought our story of Basketmaker life up to about the middle of the eighth century. We haven't told you everything about these enterprising and industrious pioneers. We haven't, for example, said much about awls and needles and other bone and horn implements, or about grinding stones, or about baby cradles, or about juniper bark torches, or about a dozen other odds and ends of their culture. We haven't had the space.

Although the Basketmakers didn't know it, they were setting the stage for the next event in southwestern prehistory, the beginning of the Pueblo Indian era.

# 6
# Early Pueblo Building Boom

With the close of the Basketmaker period we come to the Pueblo era, the second major division of the Anasazi or Ancient Ones. The name Pueblo is a Spanish word meaning village or town. It was given by the early Spaniards to Indians they found living in large, multistoried stone houses in northern Arizona and New Mexico. In the Southwest today we apply the term to these community houses and towns and to their Indian inhabitants, both prehistoric and modern.

For many years archaeologists thought that the Basketmakers and Pueblos were two entirely different peoples. When the first Basketmaker mummies were discovered more than half a century ago, it was immediately seen that their skulls were not like those of the people who had inhabited the later cliff dwellings and pueblos. Basketmaker skulls were longer and narrower and there was no cranial deformation or flattening at the back of the head as there was in Pueblo skulls.

For this reason archaeologists assumed that a new, broadheaded people had invaded the Four Corners country during the eighth century and had overthrown the Basketmakers, taking over their villages and their arts and crafts.

But now this theory has had to be tossed out the window. Recently results of detailed studies of hundreds of skeletons of both the ancient Basketmakers and the later Pueblo Indians have shown that there was, after all, little real change in physical type. There had been no invasion of a new people into the Southwest. The Basketmakers hadn't been overwhelmed and driven out of the territory.

Instead, the acquisition by the Basketmakers in the eighth century of a new item of culture resulted in a change in the shape of their heads. This item was the hard cradle board.

For hundreds, perhaps thousands, of years the Basketmakers had been using a soft padded cradle for their babies. This was made of one or two pliable hardwood sticks, bent and tied to form an oval frame 1½ to 2 feet long. Across this frame were lashed closely-spaced willow twigs, making a flexible back. This was padded with soft juniper bark and fur before the baby, wrapped in a fur-cloth blanket, was laid in it and held firmly in by cross-lashings of soft cord. Basketmaker cradles were designed for lightness and were provided with braided human hair straps so that they could be carried on the back or suspended from a tree or a house rafter to rock in the breeze.

Then suddenly a new cradle, a hard rigid board, was introduced to the Basketmakers. Where it came from we do not know. Probably it was borrowed, like so many other things, from one of the neighboring peoples.

Babies were strapped to these new cradles with no pillow between the baby's head and the wood. Day after day, week after week, the baby's soft head pressed against the hard board. As a result the back of the head gradually flattened while the sides of the skull bulged out. Actually this had no ill effects on the child except that it changed his appearance. As the bones grew and became harder, this deformation became permanent. What had once been a relatively long and narrow skull was now short and broad and flattened at the back.

For some reason this new head shape caught on and became the fashion. You weren't in style if you didn't have a deformed head. The use of the hard cradle board spread throughout the Four Corners country like wildfire. The old padded cradles were thrown on the village refuse heap and in a very short time every Basketmaker woman had herself one of the new wooden cradles.

Within a generation or two the Basketmakers had completely changed their physical appearance — and all as the result of the adoption of a new baby cradle. It is no wonder that archaeologists had been baffled.

But even though there had been no real change in physical type, there were numerous other changes that did take place in the Four Corners country during the eighth and ninth centuries. This early Pueblo period was a time of transition, of experimentation, of gradual development.

With fields of corn, beans, and squash now furnishing the people with an assured food supply, with the added security of settled village life, and with the general improvement in living conditions, the population grew rapidly. The caves were abandoned as the people moved out onto the open mesa tops and ridges and even down into broad valleys.

Caves now seem to have been used only for storage and not too often for that. As one archaeologist has so aptly said, "Cave sites of the early Pueblos are as rare as the proverbial hen's teeth."

Fig. 27. Early Pueblo masonry storage rooms in cave in north-eastern Arizona.

Fig. 28. Early Pueblo diorama at Mesa Verde National Park, Colorado.

But these Pueblo storage bins found in caves were unlike the earlier Basketmaker slab-lined pits. They foreshadow the coming styles in Pueblo architecture, consisting of small surface chambers of rectangular or oval form with walls of masonry laid in heavy mud mortar. Some were even two stories in height.

Perhaps the most important change during this time was the boom in building, not only new villages but also new styles of architecture.

When we left the Basketmakers, most of them were living in pithouses of one kind or another. Grouped around them were storage granaries constructed of stone slabs or crude masonry and mud. In most areas south of the Four Corners the pithouse remained the usual form of dwelling well into the Pueblo period.

But up in southwestern Colorado and southeastern Utah a few groups of early Pueblo Indians had begun to experiment with their storage rooms. These were small at first, with floors only slightly below ground level. Then the Indians enlarged them to house size, generally lining the walls below ground with slabs of stone and forming the rest of the walls with upright poles plastered with mud. These were capped with a flat roof of poles and mud. Once rooms became fully rectangular, with vertical side walls, it wasn't long before some inventive individual figured out that two rooms could now be built side by side, with one wall serving both rooms. This was a great labor-saving device and the idea was quickly adopted by neighboring groups.

Before too many years a village consisted of a number of these rectangular rooms joined together in a long, sometimes crescent-shaped row, generally facing the south or southeast. Thus was the Southwest's first apartment house born.

In front of this row of houses were one or two of the old-style pithouses. The photograph in this chapter shows one of these under construction and, to the right, the ends of a ladder sticking out of the hatchway of a second. But these were no longer dwelling places. When the storage bins were enlarged into living quarters, the people didn't change their religion to conform to the new style in architecture. Instead, they retained their circular underground rooms as ceremonial houses, perhaps as symbols of their original houses, perhaps also in the belief that it put them closer to the Earth Mother from whom they came.

As also indicated in the photograph, storage bins and turkey pens were grouped in back of the row of houses. Even though small side doorways, facing south into the open courtyard, were now common, many houses still had smoke-hole roof entrances. Since many of the ordinary household tasks seem to have been performed on the flat sunny roofs, hatchway entrances would have furnished easier access to these work areas.

The next architectural advance came when houses became true surface structures and masonry walls replaced the stone slabs and poles and mud of the earlier houses. We can't give the exact date when this event first took place. It didn't happen at the same time all over the Four Corners country. In some areas people began to build houses on top of the ground while they were still using pole and mud walls. In other areas walls were laid up of masonry while floors were still being dug 6 inches to a foot below ground level. However, we do know that many villages were being constructed in this new style by the opening decades of the tenth century.

Typical of these are several small villages excavated by

Fig. 29. Early Pueblo unit-type structure in eastern Arizona.

the Smithsonian Institution in Whitewater Valley in eastern Arizona. Two of the three sites uncovered had floors slightly below the surface while the third was built directly on ground level. All three had horizontally laid masonry walls and all had underground ceremonial houses in the courtyard in front.

The middle one of the three villages was probably built in the early part of the tenth century, roughly fifty years after the first and a hundred years before the third unit. It consisted of a double tier of six rooms arranged in a rectangular block, four in the back row and two in front. Three of these were definitely living rooms, containing fireplaces and storage bins. The other three smaller chambers had no such features and may have been storage rooms.

A few feet in front of the block of rooms, to the southeast, was a circular ceremonial pithouse. From now on we shall call these ceremonial chambers "kivas," the term used by archaeologists. Kiva is an ancient Hopi Indian word meaning, according to some authorities, "old house." Kivas are still found among the present-day pueblos of northern Arizona and New Mexico where they are used primarily for various rituals and as men's clubhouses for ceremonial societies. We can conjecture that these prehistoric kivas served much the same purposes.

This particular kiva was roughly circular in shape and had a bench encircling it. It was nearly 19 feet in diameter above the bench and 15 feet at floor level. It had been dug down from 5 to 6 feet below the original surface of the ground. Although the builders had used upright stone slabs for part of the foundation, they had formed the rest of the walls of stone blocks laid up in mud mortar. Covering the structure had been a cribbed roof of logs, poles, brush, and clay. Entrance was effected by means of a ladder through the smoke-hole hatchway in the center of the roof.

In the floor of the kiva were the same features we saw in late Basketmaker ceremonial pithouses — a stone-lined

Fig. 30. Kiva in early Pueblo village in eastern Arizona.

firepit with a raised rim on the southeast side representing the deflector, a sipapu, a ventilator shaft opening below floor level, and an ash pit.

The kiva also had one additional feature we haven't seen before. This was a rectangular hole lined with small stone slabs set back into the wall of the bench on the side of the room opposite the ventilator. Similar small niches are found in many modern pueblo kivas. The Hopis call it the Kachina niche, the house of the Kachinas. The Kachinas are masked impersonations of supernatural beings who are thought to live on the San Francisco Mountains near Flagstaff, Arizona. Today the visitor to the Southwest can even buy a colorful, feathered kachina doll carved from wood by the Hopi and Zuñi Indians.

Beyond the kiva, still further to the southeast, lay the village dump. Here the Pueblo women threw the ashes from their fireplaces, their broken pots and pans, their worn-out sandals, and all their other trash. In this refuse heap, perhaps because of the easier digging, the people put their burials, not only of humans but also of dogs and turkeys. Scattered over the surface of the refuse mound and around the houses were half a dozen stone-lined fireplaces and the remains of several brush shelters. These may have been used as outdoor cooking areas during the warm summer months, perhaps also serving as social gathering places.

If this six-room pueblo seems rather small for a village, even smaller ones have been found. Up in Colorado, at Mesa Verde National Park, archaeologists excavated a village of only two surface rooms built of slabs and poles and mud, a kiva, and three outside fireplaces. The kiva, a few feet southeast of the two rooms, was dug down into hard adobe soil that needed no masonry lining to keep out loose dirt or to support the roof. Yet it had a bench, firepit, deflector stone, ventilator, and a small depression that may have served as the sipapu, the opening to the underworld. Fragments of charcoal from a floor pit gave tree ring dates in the middle of the tenth century.

However, many of these early pueblos built during the tenth century contained twenty or more rooms. One such larger structure was excavated in Chaco Canyon, New Mexico, by a team from the University of New Mexico. It consisted of twenty living rooms arranged on the top of a low mound in a long double row. The walls were of roughly squared sandstone blocks set in mud and chinked with chips, pebbles, and broken pieces of pottery. The interior walls had been coated with heavy plaster. Rooms were entered by small side doorways averaging 3 feet high by 18 inches wide, each with a well-worn sill and lintel.

A beam from one of the rooms gave a tree ring date of 922 plus an estimated ten to twenty years of rings that had been worn away from the outside of the log. This would indicate that the pueblo was built about 940 or 950 A.D.

In front of this compact dwelling were four small underground kivas built of masonry. All four had benches, firepits, deflector stones or screens, and ventilating shafts. Small holes that may have been sipapus were found in at least three of the kivas. Two also had a raised masonry platform forming a southern extension. The inner walls of the kivas had been plastered, one showing fourteen distinct layers of fine adobe, each perhaps representing an annual spring housecleaning. In another the plaster coating below the bench had been covered with a series of incised designs. There were also traces of black and white paint on another section of plaster in this same kiva.

The spot where this structure was located must have been a good one in prehistoric times. Before the excavators were finished, they discovered that the pueblo had been built on top of a still older pueblo. This had been a small masonry building with an unknown number of adjoining rooms. Walls were constructed of large sandstone slabs set upright around the sides of the room, with crude masonry on top of them. The archaeologists were unable to determine the extent of this earlier structure since this would have meant complete destruction of the upper building. The first pueblo was probably built somewhere around the middle of the ninth century, perhaps a hundred years before the later pueblo was erected on its ruins.

By the end of the early Pueblo period these multiroomed masonry structures, which we call unit-type houses, had become standard over most of the Four Corners country. On the average they contained from six to twenty rooms, usually one story in height. The rooms were sometimes arranged in a straight line, sometimes in a double tier, sometimes in the shape of the letter L or U. In front of a unit-type house, generally to the south or southeast, were one or more kivas.

On the foundation laid down by the Basketmakers the Pueblos had developed a new architectural style, a style which was still a long way from the heights it was to reach over the next few centuries.

# 7
# Early Pueblo Improvements

Architecture wasn't the only field in which these early Pueblo people experimented. New styles, new fashions, and new designs were introduced into practically every one of their arts and industries.

However, the picture we present of the arts and crafts of these people is much more one-sided than was the picture of the Basketmakers'. When the early Pueblo people deserted the caves to move out into the wide open spaces, they practically destroyed whatever chance archaeologists might have had of finding out about their basketry, textiles, clothing, wooden implements and utensils, and all of their other objects made of perishable materials. About some of these things all we can do is guess.

But such was not the case with pottery. Pottery is permanent, lasting almost forever. Pots and jars break easily and are thrown out on the village dump. There they lie for century after century, never decaying, never changing, ready to speak their story to the first archaeologist who digs them up. From such small fragments, called potsherds, he can tell what they were part of — a jar, a bowl, a pitcher.

Even the fact that pots are fragile is of value because that means they have to be replaced often. Just as we are today, the prehistoric peoples of the Southwest were addicted to fads and fancies in pots and pans. New styles, new forms, and new designs had their brief moment of glory and then as quickly vanished from the market.

We didn't see too much of this in the previous period as the Basketmakers hadn't been making pots long enough to do much experimenting with their products. But the early Pueblo potters were different. Unhampered by centuries of tradition and convention, yet fully acquainted with their wares, they let their imaginations run wild, manufacturing pottery in a wide variety of shapes and sizes and in an equally wide variety of designs.

Pots were made by hand, as they still are by the present-day Pueblo Indians. The potter's wheel, invented in the Old World more than 5,000 years ago, was unknown in prehistoric America. Among the modern Pueblo Indians pottery making has always been considered woman's work and that was probably true also in early Pueblo times.

Early Pueblo pots were made by a process of coiling and scraping. After the clay had been gathered, a tempering material had to be added to reduce shrinkage and lessen the danger of cracking while the vessels were drying and during the firing process. At first sand was used as temper. Later sand was replaced by powdered rock, and still later, near the end of the early Pueblo period, by ground-up potsherds. Finally water was mixed with the clay and temper and kneaded to form a pliable paste.

The potter was then ready to begin her day's work. To start a vessel, a handful of wet clay was formed into a saucer-shaped disk. This would be the bottom or base of the new pot. The bases or bottoms of many of the first pots seem to have been molded in baskets. To the top of this saucer-shaped disk of clay a rolled-out loop of clay, about an inch in thickness, was pressed with the fingers to make a tight bond. A second loop was added and pinched to the preceding loop, then another and another until the sides were built up to the desired height and shape. A piece of gourd or wood or broken pot served as a scraper to smooth the surfaces, thus obliterating the junctions of the overlapping coils and thinning the vessel walls.

Along in early Pueblo times longer and longer loops of clay began to be used. Eventually the entire pot was made from one long clay loop coiled spirally around and around the vessel.

After the pots had been slowly dried, those that were to be decorated were coated with a wash of fine clay, known as the slip, and polished with a smooth pebble. Designs were painted on freehand with yucca leaf brushes, ground-up minerals and the juice of plants serving as paints. To harden the vessels, they were fired by piling wood around and over them and setting fire to the dome-shaped heap.

From beginning to end Pueblo pottery making was a slow, exacting process. It couldn't be hurried. Any one of a number of accidents, particularly during firing, could happen to ruin a whole day's work.

Early Pueblo potters kept pace with Pueblo architects by developing new styles and shapes and designs. They worked with finer clays and made better vessels. The differences between culinary or cooking pots and those used for other purposes became wider and wider.

Vessels were made in a greater variety of shapes than ever before — large and small cooking pots, pitchers of all sizes,

Fig. 31. Pueblo corrugated cooking jar.

Fig. 32. Early Pueblo black-on-white pottery from northeastern Arizona.

cooking bowls with side handles, storage and water jars, often with perforated side lugs for easier carrying, food bowls, ladles, and bird-shaped vessels.

In the early part of the period potters left unsmoothed the flat coils of clay on the necks of many of their jars and pitchers, giving them a banded effect. Later they began leaving the entire vessel rough, the spiral coils making alternate ridges and depressions. By pinching or indenting these coils with the finger or a stick, patterns could be formed. This type of pottery is called corrugated. In many of these vessels you can still see the fingerprints of the women who pressed the coils together a thousand years ago.

Over most of the Four Corners country the decorated pottery had black designs on a grayish-white or white background. Designs were still comparatively simple but they were better drawn than those of the Basketmakers. But before the period closed, slips or washes of fine clay gave vessels smoother finishes and designs became bigger and bolder.

In some areas a few pots were decorated with black designs on a red, sometimes orange, background. Some bowls even had polished black interiors and red or brown exteriors. These types may represent influences from the Mogollon region.

Pottery was now manufactured in such quantity that it replaced basketry for many purposes. However, several different kinds of baskets were still made and used. In the handful of caves where early Pueblo peoples briefly lived or buried their dead, a number of baskets have been found. These include carrying baskets with red and black designs and twilled ring baskets.

There were also important changes in clothing. Some of

these were due to the introduction of a new fiber into the Four Corners country. This was cotton, acquired, as you may have already guessed, from the Mogollon people. Probably the first cotton was obtained by trade as pieces of cloth. But it wouldn't have been long before the Pueblo Indians saw the advantages of this new plant and began growing their own. Along with cotton came the techniques of spinning and loom weaving.

Since textiles don't last too long in villages built out on the open ridges, we don't have much information about the types of clothing that may have been woven of cotton thread. From a burial in a cave in Segie Canyon archaeologists did recover two samples. One was a sleevelike object that may have been part of a garment, the other a small fragment of what was perhaps a robe. We can conjecture that probably cotton breechcloths were woven for men and aprons for women.

Both fur and feather robes were still made and used as cold-weather blankets and as wrappings for the dead.

The scallop-toed sandal of late Basketmaker times went out of style. Taking its place was the rounded or pointed-toed sandal. Although this type had also been made by the Basketmakers, it didn't become popular until after the opening of the new period. Many were finely woven of yucca fiber, with raised patterns on the sole, but many others were coarsely woven of heavy yucca cord.

Hair was probably worn long by both men and women. However, we do know that at least some women gathered their long hair into two bobs or knots, one on either side of the head. These knobs were wrapped with fiber cord. A burial of an eighteen-year-old woman found in a cave in Segie Canyon tells us this. As further proof, a number of

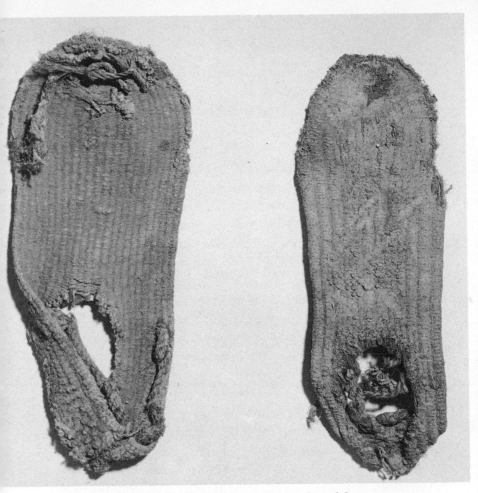

Fig. 33. Early Pueblo round-toed sandals.

early Pueblo pictographs show figures with this same style of hairdressing.

These early Pueblo Indians hadn't lost their love for ornaments. Jewelry was worn by both men and women. Bracelets, bead necklaces, pendants, ear pendants, buttons, and rings seem to have been the most common. The presence of glycymeris shell bracelets and olivella shell beads indicate that trade in shell was still brisk. Beads were made of shell, bone, and several kinds of stone, including turquoise and alabaster. A few stone pendants have been found carved in the shape of birds. Inlays and mosaics were also probably still made.

Cotton was the only new addition to the list of cultivated plants. Corn, beans, and squash remained the staple foods. But cultivation of fields was now made easier by the invention or borrowing of the stone hoe. This was made by knocking chips or flakes off a river boulder or sandstone slab to form rough notches and a flat edge or blade. Hafted to a wooden handle, this would have made a much more efficient tool than the digging stick for breaking up the ground. Similarly made pointed stone picks probably came in handy in digging the deep pits for kivas.

Both meat and wild plant foods were still included in the diet, although hunting and collecting were rapidly becoming of secondary importance to the growing of corn, beans, and squash. The bow and arrow were now used over nearly all of the Four Corners country. Among the animals hunted were rabbits, deer, antelope, elk, mountain sheep, bear, and prairie dogs. The bones of many of these animals were cut and shaped into awls, needles, scrapers, spatulas, punches, chisels, flaking tools, knife handles, whistles, gaming counters, and ornaments.

Dogs and turkeys were the only domestic animals. Although turkeys may have been occasionally eaten, they were still kept primarily for their feathers. Both dogs and turkeys are often found buried in refuse heaps adjacent to the pueblos. That these were intentional burials is shown by the frequent placing of offerings with them, small pottery vessels and corn for the turkeys, animal bones for the dogs.

A new type of grinding stone was now manufactured for the first time, supplementing the old style which continued to be used. During Basketmaker times corn had been ground on a slab of stone shaped like a trough, with one end open and the other closed. The new kind was also troughed, but it had both ends open. These milling stones were generally made of sandstone and ranged from 1½ to 2 feet in length and from 1 to 1½ feet in width.

Such grinding stones are called metates, the word coming from the Aztec Indians of Mexico. Metates are still used today to grind corn and seeds or nuts by many peoples in

Fig. 34. Early Pueblo trough-shaped metates.

Mexico and by most Indian tribes in Arizona and New Mexico.

The hand stone rubbed back and forth on the metate to crush the corn is called a mano, from the Spanish word for hand. Manos were small slabs of sandstone pecked to a rectangular shape to fit inside the trough of the metate.

No early Pueblo Indian household was considered well equipped unless it had at least one metate and two or three assorted manos.

With the upsurge in building, grooved stone axes became one of the principal tools. These could, of course, have been used as effectively to crack skulls as to fell trees. But, although an occasional broken head has been found in a burial, there does not appear to have been much fighting between villages.

Tubular stone and clay pipes, or cloud blowers as they are frequently called, continued to be manufactured. In certain Pueblo Indian ceremonies today priests using similarly shaped pipes blow smoke to the four quarters of the compass. It is possible these early Pueblo pipes were used for much the same purpose. A number of the clay pipes had a small molded figure of what appears to be a frog stuck on the side. Modern Pueblo Indians regard the frog as closely tied in with rain and rain-making practices. Rain, of course, was extremely important to these desert dwellers. Without it, there would have been no crops.

Both clay and stone were also used to make jar stoppers or plugs. Storage jars were often sealed by pressing a lump of wet clay into the mouth of the pot. For a temporary cover for a jar or a bowl, the Pueblo Indians chipped and ground thin sandstone slabs into roughly circular pot lids.

Now that the Pueblo Indians were living in permanent towns, they began to use definite places to bury their dead.

Graves were usually dug in the refuse heaps located fifty to a hundred feet south or southeast of the pueblo. You could hardly call this a cemetery as there were no grave markers and burials were scattered throughout the trash mound.

The Pueblo Indians meant no disrespect for the dead in this. The refuse heap, with its accumulated dust, ashes, broken bits of pottery, discarded animal bones, and other household debris, just happened to be the handiest and easiest place to dig.

From the few burials that have been discovered in protected caves and rock shelters, we can assume that many grave pits were lined with mats of rushes or yucca fiber. On these the body, wrapped in a fur or feather or cotton blanket, was laid in a more or less flexed or folded position. Around the body were placed offerings of pottery, basketry, clothing, implements and utensils, and food. Sometimes graves were covered with large sandstone slabs, sometimes with a pole, brush, and bark roof.

Infants and small children were often buried under the floors of houses close to the firepits. This perhaps reflects the belief common among many peoples that, even after death, a child still needs its mother's care and protection. This also insured that the family circle remained unbroken.

Burials of both adults and children were also sometimes made in old storage pits or in abandoned rooms in the pueblos.

One early Pueblo burial from a cave site in northern Arizona illustrates the amount of perishable material that was sometimes buried with the dead. This was the grave of the eighteen-year-old woman with the unique hair-do. The bottom of the grave had been covered with rush mats. The body had been wrapped in fur-string robes and also in some type of cotton cloth. Over the body was a large coiled carrying basket. Other offerings included several pieces of plain and decorated pottery, fragments of a sandal, a sleeve-like cotton object, a broken bow and part of another bow, a woven strap, part of a firedrill, and a quantity of corncobs. The grave had been roofed over with poles, reeds, and bark.

Another unusual grave was discovered near an early Pueblo shallow pit village in southwestern Colorado. It was called the Arrowmaker Burial because twenty-two excellently chipped arrowheads were found with the body. In addition, there were bone-flaking tools, a pile of stone flakes, twenty-one pieces of pottery, red paint, a paint-mixing palette, and the bones of a golden eagle.

Like the Basketmaker burial of the hands, a number of queer early Pueblo burials have also been reported. Occasionally a headless skeleton turns up in a burial ground. Occasionally a skull is found without a body.

In the refuse mound of a small village in southwestern Colorado archaeologists excavated one of these puzzling burials. In a small circular pit dug into the ground below the refuse were two male heads and a few neck bones. Filling the rest of the pit were four pottery bowls. There were no other bones.

On top of the changes that were occurring in architecture, in pottery, in clothing, and in other arts and crafts, equally important changes were taking place in the social life of these early Pueblo people. Settled village life undoubtedly led to new social rules and regulations. People can't live closely grouped together without some type of law and order. Religion, with its accompanying ceremonies and ritual, developed into a group or community rather than an individual affair.

Although we can't dig up customs as we can pots and

pans, we can guess as to what must have been happening. Since the present-day Pueblo Indians still live much as their ancestors did a thousand years ago, we can assume that their social and religious practices were also probably similar.

A modern Pueblo community is broken down into well-defined units, called clans. Whereas we group people by families, following the male side, the Pueblos group by clan, following the female side. Every Pueblo Indian is born into one clan, the clan of his mother, and remains a member of that clan as long as he lives. When he marries, he goes to live in his wife's house, which is her property, not his.

These clans are close-knit organizations. Each has its own name, generally that of a plant or animal, controls farming sites, preserves its distinct legends, and performs its separate ceremonies in the clan or society kiva. Clans also regulate marriage by prohibiting it between members of the same clan. They are never very large, usually ranging from about forty to sixty or more members.

A Pueblo man, therefore, does not belong to the same clan as his wife or his children. His closest social and ceremonial relationships are with his mother's people, his own clan members. Perhaps that is why the average Pueblo man, an outsider in his own home, spends much of his time in the kiva. For the kiva has its social as well as its ceremonial side. The kiva also serves as a workshop for those who want to work and as a lounging place or corner club room for those who have nothing better to do than sit around and talk. Many of the older boys and men may even sleep there on occasion when they want a night out. Except on special occasion women are barred from the kivas, which are the property of the men.

In addition, cutting across the clan organization are several societies or fraternities — Kachina societies, medicine or curing societies, and warrior societies. These also have a social as well as a religious aspect. A Pueblo man might belong to all three of these societies.

By projecting this picture of Pueblo social and ceremonial life back into prehistoric times, archaeologists can better understand the meaning of many of the things they uncover. The kiva is one example.

A small unit-type community house with five or six rooms and a kiva can be explained as a one-clan or one-society group, a twenty-room structure with four kivas as a four-clan or four-society group. The great kivas that some of the late Basketmakers built might be called ceremonial structures for the entire community.

The idea of the great kiva seems to have originated in southwestern Colorado. At least more have been discovered in that region in late Basketmaker and very early Pueblo times. These were generally associated with large villages of ten to fifteen deep pithouses and a hundred or more adjoining masonry surface rooms, some used for storage, some as dwellings. Villages this size would have needed something bigger than an ordinary pithouse for ceremonial dances or festivals in which the whole village participated. Perhaps such ceremonies were put on in these great kivas by several clans or societies for the benefit of the entire village or of the surrounding smaller villages.

This is, of course, guesswork. We can't say definitely that the early Pueblo people were grouped into clans and societies and that they used kivas for the purposes indicated. But chances are good that we are right.

In the next two or three centuries after 1000 A.D. the sons and grandsons of these early Pueblo Indians were to bring about even greater changes in their architecture, their arts and industries, and their religious and social life.

# 8
# Apartment Houses and Penthouses

Pueblo Bonito, Chettro Kettle, Pueblo Alto, Hungo Pavi, Pueblo del Arroyo, Aztec, Cliff Palace, Spruce Tree House, Balcony House, Far View House, Betatakin, Keet Seel, Inscription House, Batwoman Pueblo, Poncho House, White House, Antelope House — these are just a few of the hundreds of pueblos and cliff dwellings so far discovered in the Four Corners country. For this was the Pueblo Golden Age, the era archaeologists call the Great or Classic Pueblo period.

We know far more about the life and times of this period than we do about any other. That isn't hard to understand. These ruins were huge and impressive and easy to spot. Moreover, digging in a large ruin, particularly in one in a protected cave, promised a rich haul of pottery and basketry and jewelry.

Unfortunately for science, by no means all of that digging was done by trained archaeologists. Newspaper and other accounts of the spectacular discoveries brought a flood of pot hunters pouring into the Southwest. Scores of prehistoric cliff dwellings and pueblos were vandalized. Thousands of specimens, many of them unique and irreplaceable, were literally torn from their centuries-old resting places and carted off. Finally, after nearly twenty years of such looting, laws were passed to protect all prehistoric ruins on federal land. Most of the states also enacted similar laws for ruins on state lands. Today many of the largest and most outstanding of these pueblos and cliff dwellings have been set aside as national or state parks and monuments, where they are preserved for future study and where they can be viewed by the public.

The Pueblo Golden Age began some time during the eleventh century and lasted until nearly the end of the thirteenth century. During that 300-year period the Pueblo Indians reached their peak of development in architecture and in arts and industries.

But it didn't happen all at once. Just as in the earlier periods, some groups were more conservative than others. In certain areas people continued to live in small unit-type houses much as they had in early Pueblo times. But in other regions other people, perhaps because they were more progressive, perhaps for different reasons we may never know, began to gather together in larger and larger numbers, building bigger and bigger houses to shelter the increasing population.

Great multiroomed, multistoried apartment houses sprang up on mesa tops and in the bottoms of canyons. Up in the red-rock cliffs in the heart of the Four Corners country there was even a return to the caves, These huge natural caverns which had been standing empty since the Basketmakers moved out now became beehives of building activity. In the shelter of the overhanging cliffs scores of rooms were built, often rising to a height of four stories.

These were the famous cliff dwellings or cliff houses,

built by the so-called cliff dwellers. Contrary to popular belief, these cliff dwellers were not a different race of people
from those who built their houses out in the open. They
were all Pueblo Indians, the descendants of the earlier Basketmakers and the ancestors of the modern Pueblo Indians
of Arizona and New Mexico.

The general plan of these large apartment houses, whether built in caves or in river valleys, was similar. Each pueblo
consisted of a compact block of adjoining rooms, from
twenty or so in the smallest up to nearly a thousand in the
largest. Each was from one to four or five stories in height,
the upper stories being set back in steps as is a terraced sky-
scraper. Sometimes the pueblo was built in the form of a
rectangle, sometimes an oval, or sometimes like the letter
D or E or L. In rectangular pueblos the kivas were usually
incorporated within the building itself. In others the living
rooms were grouped around an open court in which the
kivas were located. In cliff dwellings the living rooms were
built around the back wall facing the mouth of the cave,
with the kivas along the front.

Typical of many of the smaller rural or suburban villages
built during the early part of the eleventh century are two
pueblos along the Arizona-New Mexico border.

The first of these, the Village of the Great Kivas, is located south of Gallup, New Mexico, on the present-day
Zuñi Indian Reservation. It was excavated by archaeologists
from the Smithsonian Institution in the summer of 1930.
The settlement consisted of three separate structures, a large
unit to the north, a smaller unit to the west, and a still
smaller one 300 feet to the south.

The largest unit contained sixty-four rooms, sixty on the
ground floor and four on the second story, arranged in a

Fig. 35. Village of the Great Kivas on the Zuñi Indian Reservation, New Mexico.

long rectangle. Three small kivas were included within the building and there were four more along the front of the eastern wing. In one of these front kivas geometric designs had been cut into the wall plaster and then colored with a light paint. Near the center of the southern side of this unit there was a great kiva, with a second great kiva a hundred feet further to the south.

The smaller western unit contained twenty rooms arranged in a double or triple tier running north and south. The smallest unit had only six rooms in a double row east and west. There were no small kivas or ceremonial chambers with either of these two units. To the south or southeast of each of the three pueblos was a refuse mound.

This sounds like a rather large pueblo. But the excavators soon discovered that it had been built in several different stages and that not all of the rooms had been occupied at the same time. This, as we shall see, seems to have been a common practice in prehistoric times.

About 1000 A.D. a group of Pueblo Indians from the north had moved into the valley and built a rectangular block of thirteen living rooms and two circular kivas, enclosing the latter within larger square rooms and filling in the corners. A few years later they added four or five more rooms and the great kiva. This was over 50 feet in diameter above the bench and was partially below and partially above ground, with four massive masonry and wood pillars supporting the huge roof.

Later, new arrivals, probably from the south, moved in and made themselves at home, adding east and west wings to the main pueblo and digging more ceremonial rooms out in front. Some of the old rooms were abandoned and filled with trash to prevent sagging walls from collapsing. Still later, more arrivals, also from the south, built separate quarters to the west and south. Why they did this we can't say.

Some time during the occupation of the pueblo a fire destroyed the great kiva. The second one may then have been built to replace the first. It was even larger, measuring 78 feet in diameter above the masonry bench.

The excavators concluded that the village probably had had a population of about a hundred during the middle and later part of its existence. They also concluded that it had been deserted about 1030 A.D.

The second of our rural villages illustrating the building activity of the early part of the eleventh century is located in eastern Arizona about 60 miles southwest of the Village of the Great Kivas. This is the pueblo of Kiatuthlanna, meaning the "Place of the Big Water," so named by the

Zuñi Indians. Like the Village of the Great Kivas, it was excavated by the Smithsonian Institution and, like that pueblo, it shows how pueblos often grew by degrees.

The pueblo began as a small unit of six rooms forming a rectangle partially surrounding a circular kiva. Curiously the walls had been built almost entirely of adobe mud. Within a few years seven living rooms and another kiva were added on the southwest side, possibly by incoming members of a different clan. Here, too, the walls, with the exception of those of the kiva, were of adobe. In a few more years six rooms were erected on the southwest side of the second unit in the shape of an L, forming a court with one wall of that unit. But most of these new walls were of masonry, the stones for which had to be hauled by hand and foot a distance of at least 10 miles.

The next addition perhaps came about because of the abandonment of the first block of rooms. At any rate these had begun to be used as trash pits. A new kiva was built in what had been the courtyard of the third unit and six new rooms were put around it to make a solid rectangle. For some reason the builders went back to using adobe for their walls.

The final building stage came when the kiva in the second unit was destroyed by fire. This remodeling effort added twenty-one rooms and a kiva on the southeast side of the fourth unit, making an L-shaped structure. Once again the building material changed. Interior walls were still constructed of adobe, but the new outer walls were of masonry. The builders even went back and covered all the old outer adobe walls with a thin veneer of stone.

At the end of all this building activity the pueblo contained some forty living rooms and two kivas. Archaeologists couldn't tell how much longer the inhabitants continued to live there. But eventually, probably some time later in the eleventh century, they packed up and left.

Although these two pueblos, the Village of the Great Kivas and Kiatuthlanna, were fairly large for that particular time and location, they were completely dwarfed by the huge building boom that was taking place nearer the heart of the Four Corners country. Three areas led the way in this spectacular development, each serving as a cultural center from which influence spread out over a wide region. These were Chaco Canyon in northwestern New Mexico, Mesa Verde in southwestern Colorado, and Kayenta in northeastern Arizona.

Chaco Canyon was not only the first pueblo area to enter the Classic Period but it also produced the largest and most impressive buildings. In an area little more than 8 miles long and 2 miles wide there are more than a dozen large pueblos and scores of smaller ones. Archaeologists have estimated that the combined population of these towns, assuming that most of them were occupied at the same time, must have been between 15,000 and 25,000.

Today, looking at this almost barren, red-walled, sandy-floored canyon, we wonder how it could have supported so many people. But of that, more later.

The largest and the most famous prehistoric ruin in Chaco Canyon is Pueblo Bonito, the Spanish words for "beautiful village." This colossal structure may not have been the Southwest's first apartment house but it was certainly the biggest.

The back-country Indian visitor of 1100 A.D., catching his first glimpse of Pueblo Bonito from the rim of the canyon, must have thought the whole of the civilized world lay at his feet.

Even now, its ruins cleared of the dust and debris of centuries, it is an impressive sight. A thousand years ago it must have been even more so. Covering more than three acres of ground, it stood four stories in height and contained over 800 rooms and 32 kivas. Arranged in a huge D-shape, its straight south-facing wall measured 518 feet in length. From this one-story front with its two open courtyards full of kivas, the rooms rose in terraced steps to the four-story-high curving rear wall. At the peak of its glory Pueblo Bonito probably housed 1200 people.

Fig. 36. Pueblo Bonito in Chaco Canyon National Monument, New Mexico.

— *National Park Service*

Like most pueblos, Pueblo Bonito wasn't built in one giant construction operation. It grew in stages. Tree ring dates from ancient roof beams reveal that people were living on this spot as early as 919 A.D. These first settlers seem to have been Anasazi immigrants from north of the San Juan River in southern Utah and Colorado. The decorations on their kitchenware and the styles of their stone architecture tell us so. Why they wandered this far afield before staking out a claim is a mystery. The pueblo they built consisted of a double row of rectangular rooms in a crescent facing southeast, with at least three sunken kivas in front.

Then, early in the eleventh century, a new group of immigrants from north of the San Juan invaded the valley. They liked what they saw and moved in on the original inhabitants, adding more rooms right and left. These later Bonitians were less old-fashioned, more progressive than the original settlers. Seemingly outnumbering the latter, they embarked on an ambitious building program, twice enlarging the pueblo and making extensive alterations. They became expert workers in stone, erecting perhaps the finest walls in the entire Southwest. The latest and best walls were massive, consisting of a core of stone and rubble faced on either side with a veneer of thin flat slabs of sandstone, carefully shaped and fitted together so closely they needed very little mud mortar.

By the last quarter of the eleventh century Pueblo Bonito probably had reached its final form. In 1130 A.D., according to a tree ring date, the Bonitians did a small job of restoration. So far as we know that was the end of building. How long a time after that the pueblo continued to be occupied we don't know, but archaeologists believe it wasn't too long, They think the descendants of the original settlers hung on for a few years after the late Bonitians pulled out.

Pueblo Bonito was only one of many such towns in Chaco Canyon. Less than a quarter of a mile to the west was another apartment house, Pueblo del Arroyo, its Spanish name referring to its location beside a deep wash or gully. This was considerably smaller than Pueblo Bonito, but it was still huge by eleventh-century standards. Like Pueblo Bonito it was partially excavated by archaeologists sponsored by the National Geographic Society. They estimated that it had contained a total of 284 rooms arranged in a rectangular block, with two one-story curving wings enclosing an open court and forming an overall D-shaped structure. Of these rooms 120 were on the ground floor, 86 on the second floor, 64 on the third, and possibly 14 on a fourth story. In addition, there were at least 17 ceremonial chambers or kivas within the walls.

Pueblo del Arroyo was built and occupied when Pueblo Bonito was at its height. Tree rings from thirty-one beams show dates ranging from 1052 to 1117 A.D.

Less than half a mile on the opposite side of Pueblo Bonito, up the valley to the east, was still another large pueblo, Chettro Kettle. This five-story, D-shaped apartment house had contained over 500 rooms and had been built during the years from 1030 to 1116 A.D.

All along Chaco Canyon were still more of these large two-, three-, and four-story pueblos, all having been constructed during the eleventh and early twelfth centuries. Each had its quota of smaller, circular clan or society kivas and some also had great kivas. At Pueblo Bonito there was one 60 feet in diameter, while Chettro Kettle had one several feet larger.

Fig. 37. Chettro Kettle pueblo in Chaco Canyon National Monument, New Mexico.

Digging on down beneath the great kiva at Chettro Kettle, archaeologists from the University of New Mexico and the School of American Research discovered an even earlier amphitheater-like structure built of excellent masonry. In the lower walls the excavators found ten sealed niches. In each had been placed such offerings as shell and onyx beads, pendants and buttons of turquoise. In all they recovered more than 17,000 beads and 100 pieces of turquoise.

Across the wash from Pueblo Bonito was a still larger great kiva. Since there were only a few rooms surrounding this great kiva, archaeologists think it may have been a religious center for some of the smaller pueblos in the vicinity.

From the number of great kivas occurring in Chaco Canyon, the Pueblo Indians of the eleventh century may well have considered this a ceremonial center as well as a center for trade.

Smaller kivas also played their part in Chaco Canyon social and ceremonial life. Even though they were generally erected inside of the block of houses, they were still circular and, in effect, still subterranean. This was produced by building them inside a larger rectangle of walls and filling the space between with rubble and masonry. The flat roofs of many kivas even formed dooryards for residents of second- and third-story houses. The strong influence that religion had is shown by the way living rooms were often torn down to make way for the construction of new kivas.

Kivas were better built and more complicated in their interior arrangements. Most kivas ranged from 15 to 30 feet in diameter and, though usually lacking sipapus, were equipped with benches, fireplaces, ventilators, and deflectors. Many had six wooden or stone pillars, called pilasters, built up several feet from the top of the bench to support a cribbed log roof. Sacrificial offerings of shells and turquoise beads and pendants were placed at the top of each pilaster in a special hole covered with a wooden or stone disk. Walls were whitewashed or plastered with a coating of fine clay, twenty such layers being counted in one kiva.

The typical Chaco Canyon household consisted of an all-purpose living room and one or more storage rooms. In general, ground-floor rooms were used for storage, with residential quarters on the better-lighted second, third, and fourth stories. Abandoned lower-floor rooms were often used as convenient dumping places for trash from the upper rooms. Windows were unknown to these Pueblo builders, all light having to come in through front doors or roof hatchways.

Most rooms averaged about 12 to 13 or 14 feet in size, with ceilings 7 to 8 feet high. Normally living-room walls were plastered while those in storerooms were not. Also, living rooms were usually furnished with a stone-lined fireplace.

Whenever possible, housewives probably carried on their daily chores out of doors — on the terraced roofs in front of their apartments or in the courtyard below.

Doorways were rectangular or T-shaped, 2 feet wide and 3½ to 4 feet high, with their sills from 1 to 2 feet above floor level. Roof hatchway entrances were about 2 feet wide and 3 feet long. Storeroom doorways were usually provided with secondary lintels and jambs to support stone door slabs. But other doorways seemingly remained open.

These doorways connected interior rooms or opened out on the first-, second-, or third-story roofs. There were few doors in the ground-floor opening to the outside of the pueblo. At Pueblo Bonito, for example, there were no outside doors on the curving back wall. The Bonitians had left a gate in the front wall, but eventually they even walled that up. After that every man, woman, and child entering or leaving the pueblo had to climb a ladder, cross the rooftops of the one-story houses enclosing the court, and go down a ladder on the other side.

This can only be interpreted as a defensive measure to keep out unwanted intruders. But it doesn't tell us against whom such a defense was needed. Archaeologists haven't been able to find any traces of warlike nomadic tribes in the area as early as the eleventh or twelfth centuries. They might, of course, have been other Pueblo Indian groups. In either case no good evidences of warfare have been found. We just don't know the answer.

One very real danger did, however, menace the inhabitants of Pueblo Bonito. Not far behind the town rose the sheer sandstone wall of the canyon. A huge section of this cliff had broken away from the main rock wall and now hung there, precariously balanced, threatening at any moment to topple down upon the pueblo. To prevent this frightful calamity, the Bonitians built a brace of logs and stones beneath the foot of the rock where wind and water were beginning to undercut it. For this reason the Navaho Indians call Pueblo Bonito the "place where the rock is braced up."

Though it is doubtful whether this tiny brace did much to keep the 30,000 or more tons of rock from falling, it probably did allay the fears of the Bonitians. At least Threatening Rock neved toppled during their stay in the canyon. In fact the rock remained upright for some 800 years before it finally came crashing down on January 22, 1941, damaging 100 feet of the back wall of the pueblo and twenty-one adjoining rooms.

To climb up these cliffs to the mesa tops above, the residents of Pueblo Bonito and most of the other large pueblos cut stairways in the solid rock in back of their towns. Some of these ancient stairways are still used today.

Why the Bonitians and other Pueblo dwellers in Chaco Canyon packed up and left in the twelfth century is still another question we can't definitely answer. But archaeologists reason somewhat along the following lines.

Pueblo Bonito, Chettro Kettle, Pueblo del Arroyo, and all the other pueblos in Chaco Canyon were built and occupied by farmers. When these people migrated into the valley a thousand years ago, Chaco Canyon could not have looked as it does today. Obviously it must have possessed all four of the Pueblo necessities of life — water, farming land, timber, and building stone — or they would never have settled there.

The tremendous building boom of the last half of the eleventh century took literally thousands upon thousands of logs for roof beams alone. Those recovered from the ruins show they had been cut within easy hauling distance. Today a handful of trees, some living, some dead, standing 15 miles away represent the sole survivors of this once extensive forest. Without these trees to check run-off water after heavy storms, soil was washed away and deep gullies soon formed. As the water table lowered, springs and trees and shrubs all dried up and farming became more and more difficult. Unable to raise sufficient food, the Indians were forced to leave in search of greener pastures.

While we can't say that this theory is correct, it seems to fit the facts. We do know that the abandonment was deliberate, carried out over a period of years. There are no signs of hurry or haste. People left little behind them.

Tree ring dates indicate that this withdrawal began shortly after 1100 and continued for the next thirty or forty years. Some of the refugees may have gone south, others east, still others west. A considerable number found water and farming lands 60 miles north of Chaco Canyon along the Animas River. There they settled down and, between 1106 and 1121 A.D., built a 500-room, three-story apartment house surrounding a courtyard. In addition to a number of small kivas, they constructed a great kiva 48 feet in diameter within the plaza.

This great kiva, which has since been reconstructed, was an extraordinary structure. Instead of one bench it had two, one above the other. Supporting the heavy roof beams were four massive pillars built up of wood and stone. In the floor were two huge stone-lined vaults. Similar sub-floor vaults have been found in great kivas in Chaco Canyon and at the Village of the Great Kivas, but their exact purpose is not known. Between the southern ends of these vaults was a raised masonry box which may have been a fire altar. On the south side, opening into the kiva, was an alcove with a stone altar in the center. This alcove is believed to have served as a shrine room. Surrounding the kiva was a ring of

Fig. 38. Reconstructed kiva and corner of main Pueblo at Aztec National Monument, New Mexico.

— *National Park Service*

arc-shaped rooms built at ground level, each with an open-ing into the main kiva. These seem to have been ceremonial chambers, not living quarters.

The nineteenth-century discoverers of this ruin named it Aztec, believing it had been built by the Aztec Indians of Mexico. Although we now know its inhabitants were Pueblo Indians, the name has stuck. It was excavated by the American Museum of Natural History and is today pro-tected and preserved as a national monument.

How much longer after 1121 the Chaco Canyon refugees remained at Aztec is another unsolved mystery. We do know that influences and immigrants from the Mesa Verde country to the north dominated the valley before 1200 A.D.

Wherever the ex-Chaco Canyon dwellers went next, they seem to have hidden their tracks. At least archaeologists haven't been able to find their distinctive styles of archi-tecture and pottery in any of the ruins that have been ex-cavated. Perhaps they split up into small groups and merged with other Pueblo Indians, adopting the architecture and arts and crafts of their new neighbors.

# 9
# Cliff
# Dweller Country

North of Chaco Canyon and Aztec, in southwestern Colorado, southeastern Utah, and northeastern Arizona, lies cliff dweller country, the home of the prehistoric Mesa Verde and Kayenta peoples.

Mesa Verde is Spanish for "green tableland," an appropriate name for this tree-covered plateau rising like a giant table nearly 2,000 feet above the surrounding valleys. Because of the multitude of cliff dwellings and other ruins on this mesa, it has been set aside and protected as Mesa Verde National Park. From this center Mesa Verde culture extended its influence over a wide area surrounding the Four Corners.

Large and small cliff dwellings, two-, three-, and four-story pueblos on the mesa or out in the valleys, square towers, round towers, oval towers, triple-walled structures, painted kivas, even great kivas — the Mesa Verde region had them all.

Although Mesa Verde is famous for its cliff dwellings, these came late in the Great Pueblo period. At the opening of the eleventh century most Pueblo people in the Mesa

129

Verde country were living in small, one-, or two-story, unit-type pueblos widely scattered over the mesa and down in the neighboring valleys. By the opening of the next century these small villages had started banding together to construct larger apartment houses. The kivas, which had been located outside the pueblos to the south, were now built inside the villages, either surrounded by masonry house walls or in walled-in courtyards.

Far View House, built on top of Mesa Verde, is a good example of these twelfth-century pueblos. This was a rectangular block of some fifty living rooms and five kivas, with an enclosed court on the south side. It was terraced, rising from one story on the south to three stories at the back. There were no external doorways. Nearly a score of similar pueblos lie in ruins in the immediate vicinity, and there are dozens of others here and there over the top of the mesa.

Within another century, by the late 1100's, most of these large pueblos had been abandoned. Some of their inhabitants migrated southward to Aztec where they reoccupied the empty structure and built new pueblos around it. Some seemingly wandered still further eastward to join distant relatives already established in the upper Rio Grande Valley in New Mexico. Others remained behind but gathered together in still larger, more compact pueblos, usually placed around springs or other sources of permanent water. Along the Utah-Colorado border some began building towers — square, rectangular, circular, oval, and D-shaped.

These towers are spectacular, impressive, and mysterious. They were well built, of solid stone masonry, sometimes within pueblos, sometimes all alone. They were usually two stories or more in height. Many walls still stand over 20 feet above ground level. Practically all had doorways in the side, often with an additional doorway in the second story. The only other openings were what appear to be loopholes. They have been called everything from watchtowers to fortresses to ceremonial observatories.

Some towers are built on high ridges where they may well have been watchtowers or lookout posts. But others are located down in canyons where the view was limited. Many are too small to have been of any value as fortresses. Possible ceremonial use is indicated for some by the occasional presence of prayer sticks or other ceremonial offerings.

The largest and best preserved group of towers and associated pueblos is now included in the Hovenweep National Monument just west of Mesa Verde. It is named after a Ute Indian word meaning "deserted valley."

All of these happenings – the change toward larger pueblos, migrations southward and eastward, the moving of the kivas inside the pueblos, building of towers and other defensive structures – seem to show that the Mesa Verde people were faced with the need for security against some outside danger. Many archaeologists think this threat came from nomadic tribes of Indians pushing into the Southwest. But more of that in a later chapter.

To meet the danger most of the region's inhabitants retreated to the safety of Mesa Verde's rough and rugged plateau. There, in the high shallow caves open to the sunlight but protected from bad weather or enemies by overhanging sandstone cliffs, they began to build cliff dwellings.

Sun Point Pueblo illustrates this withdrawal to the canyons and also shows the resourcefulness of the Mesa Verde Indians. This was a twelfth-century pueblo of thirty rooms, with a kiva and a tower in the center of the block of rooms.

Fig. 39. Cliff Palace in Mesa Verde National Park.

When the inhabitants followed the example of their neighbors and moved to a nearby cave, they packed up everything they owned. They even tore down the walls of their houses and used the stones to build their new cliff dwelling.

No one knows exactly how many cliff dwellings there are in Mesa Verde's score of large canyons and countless smaller side canyons. Every canyon has its share of big and little caves and in nearly every one there is a ruin. So far archaeological surveys have recorded over 800 cave and ledge ruins in the park, and there are probably still more that haven't been discovered.

Cliff Palace, the largest of all the cliff ruins, was discovered in 1888 by a pair of cowboys out hunting lost cattle. Riding up to the edge of a deep narrow canyon, they spotted an enormous cave under the overhanging cliff on the opposite side. Filling the cave from end to end was a huge stone city, its walls rising all the way up to the arching roof. In their excitement the boys gave it the name Cliff Palace.

Cliff Palace isn't a palace. It was home for perhaps 400 Pueblo Indians, a big four-story apartment house containing over 200 living rooms, 23 kivas, and numerous small storage rooms. The houses were arranged in a 300-foot-long crescent hugging the back wall of the cave, with the kivas sunk in terraces along the front. There were both round and square towers, one of the latter four stories high, with mural decorations in red and white on the walls of the third story.

Rooms were generally smaller than those in pueblos built in the open and often lacked fireplaces. Mesa Verde women, like those of Chaco Canyon, must have performed most of their household tasks on the terraced rooftops or in the open courts. When the men were not out hunting or farming on the mesa above, they probably spent much of their time in their kivas.

Cliff Palace's kivas, as well as those in most other Mesa Verde cliff dwellings, represented a vast amount of hard work. Equipped only with stone tools, these Indian builders often had to dig down through solid rock to make their ceremonial chambers completely underground. Perhaps for this reason all their kivas were small, averaging about 13 feet in diameter. They didn't have the room to build great kivas.

Mesa Verde kivas were fitted out with all the usual interior fixtures of benches, six pilasters or roof supports, ventilators, deflectors, fireplaces, Kachina niches, and sipapus. Even though the latter holes sometimes had to be drilled into solid rock, nearly every kiva had one. The smooth plastered walls of one kiva were painted a bright yellow.

Less than two miles from Cliff Palace is another large cliff dwelling, Spruce Tree House, perhaps the best preserved of all. In places three stories high, Spruce Tree House had 114 living and storage rooms and eight kivas. The roof of the cave formed the roof of the third-story rooms. A court or broad street divided the town into two sections. As in Cliff Palace, rooms were entered by roof hatchways or by rectangular or T-shaped side doorways. As in many cliff dwellings, the back part of the cave had been used as a refuse dump.

Still another cliff dwelling, Square Tower House, contained sixty living rooms and eight kivas. Its most conspicuous feature is a three-story square tower standing 35 feet high. Its second-story interior walls still show the original plaster, painted red below and white above.

Fig. 40. Mesa Verde Museum diorama of Pueblo life in Spruce Tree House.

— *Mesa Verde National Park*

Balcony House illustrates how easily these cliff dwellings could be defended against enemy attack. The ruin derives its name from the well-preserved balconies or walks under the second-story doorways. Balconies, however, were not unique to this particular site. Other cliff dwellings also had them.

Balcony House was built in a picturesque cave 700 feet above the canyon floor. A solid masonry wall along the outer edge enclosed an open court at one end of the cave. This may have been built at the insistence of Cliff Dweller mothers uneasy over the possibility of their youngsters' taking a header into space. At the back of the cave was a spring of clear cold water.

The only entrance to Balcony House in prehistoric times was down a nearly vertical cliff by toe-hold steps cut in the rock. This was bad enough, but the hardest part still lay ahead, through a narrow crack in the cliff wall. Although this crack was only 3 feet wide and 25 feet long, it was still too wide for the Cliff Dwellers. They erected two stone walls, leaving a tunnel through which a person had to crawl on hands and knees. Balcony House occupants, with their own water supply, their storage rooms filled with food, and their easily defended narrow entrance, could have held off an enemy for a long time.

Most of these cliff dwellings were built and occupied during the twelfth and thirteenth centuries. Tree ring dates for Cliff Palace range from 1073 to 1273, for Square Tower House from 1066 to 1259, for Spruce Tree House from 1020 to 1274, for Oak Tree House from 1055 to 1184, for Painted Kiva House from 1199 to 1202, for Long House from 1184 to 1277, and for Balcony House from 1190 to 1279 A.D. Although some of these dates extend back into the

1000's the major construction activity didn't begin until a hundred years later.

Cliff dwellings and pueblos were not the only prehistoric buildings put up by these Mesa Verde Pueblo Indians. Watchtowers, towers with connecting kivas, fire temples, and sun temples were also built during the twelfth and thirteenth centuries.

A number of isolated watchtowers occur on the mesa. One of the largest of these was 11 feet in diameter and 25 feet in height, built against a cliff. Loopholes at different levels commanded the approaches to the tower.

Cedar Tree Tower represented a different type of tower. This 15-foot circular tower was connected to a subterranean kiva by an underground passage. The kiva had all the standard features except a sipapu. There was, however, a small hole in the center of the tower which may have served the same purpose. Just west of the kiva was a small masonry room, also connected to the kiva and tower by an underground passage. This could have been a dressing room for the men putting on ceremonies in the kiva. Although there were pueblos in the immediate vicinity, there were none close to these ceremonial buildings. This tower-kiva combination has also been found in Sun Point Pueblo on the mesa and at other sites in the neighboring valleys.

New Fire House and Fire Temple formed still another odd group of ruins in three small adjoining caves. Fire Temple may well have been what its name implies. A huge court with a circular firepit in the center was flanked at either end by two-story buildings. The walls of these rooms were plastered red and white inside and on the side facing the court and were decorated with symbolic figures. A low wall and what could have been a spectator bench closed in

Fig. 41. Fire Temple in Mesa Verde National Park.

the canyon side of the cave. Against the cliff at the back of the cave had been erected a head-high wall, also plastered red and white and decorated with zigzag markings and triangular figures.

A hundred feet to the east of Fire Temple were two other caves, one above the other, which contained a few living storage rooms and two or three circular ceremonial rooms. These were thought to have been the homes of the fire priests and their families. Tree ring dates tell us that New Fire House was occupied at least from 1153 to 1263 A.D.

Another probable religious structure is Sun Temple, located on the top of the mesa across the canyon from Cliff Palace. This remarkable surface building was D-shaped, with double walls 12 feet in height constructed of some of the finest masonry in Mesa Verde. A central plaza was surrounded by a series of rooms, with two circular ceremonial rooms in the court and another within the rooms. There was no evidence to indicate that any of the rooms were ever roofed. The absence of fireplaces and other signs of household equipment shows that the building was intended for the performance of some kind of religious rites and ceremonies.

After nearly 700 years of silence, some of Mesa Verde's cliff dwellings are again echoing with activity. For the past few years teams of archaeologists under the joint sponsorship of the National Park Service and the National Geographic Society are digging into hitherto unexplored ruins. Long House, Step House, Mug House, and other cliff dwellings are beginning to yield their long buried secrets.

South and west of Mesa Verde, over in northeastern

Arizona, another building boom was under way in the last of our three major culture centers, the Kayenta.

Like the Mesa Verde area, the Kayenta had both open pueblos and cliff dwellings. In fact, some archaeologists trace the birth of the cliff dwellings to this Kayenta region. Caves in northeastern Arizona's sandstone cliffs seem to have been occupied more or less continuously from Basketmaker days on down through the Great Pueblo period.

Even so, the latter part of the eleventh century and the early years of the twelfth century found most Kayenta people living in small pueblos in the valleys or in tiny cliff dwellings. These often consisted of only one, two, or three rooms, and the largest usually did not exceed twenty or thirty rooms.

The Pueblo Indian population of this area seems never to have been quite as dense as it was in Chaco Canyon or on Mesa Verde. By the close of the twelfth century some Kayenta people appear to have migrated southward and eastward to better watered country.

The people who stayed behind began to desert their small pueblos and gather into larger and larger apartment houses. Pueblos in the canyons or out in the valleys ranged up to a hundred and more rooms. Cliff dwellings also increased in size.

Kayenta architecture is totally different from that of either Chaco Canyon or Mesa Verde. Round towers are absent, as are also great kivas.

Pueblos in the open were generally arranged in a single or double row of one- or two-story rooms. In front of the house block were circular subterranean kivas. These had firepits, ventilators, and deflectors but lacked the pilasters or pillars of Mesa Verde kivas.

Fig. 42. Wattlework wall in Betatakin cliff dwelling.

Fig. 43. Keet Seel cliff dwelling in northern Arizona.
— *National Park Service*

Kayenta masonry was generally inferior to any we have so far seen. Walls were frequently built up of irregular or odd-shaped stones, with the use of large amounts of mud mortar. The builders seem to have made little selection of their stones, picking up whatever was handy. If the rocks didn't fit properly, they filled in with mud. Wattlework walls, built of upright poles and sticks liberally coated with mud, were relatively common in cliff dwellings.

Kayenta cliff dwellings even look different. Most caves in this area are more rock shelters than real caves, with steeply sloping floors. These make one- or two-story rooms look like terraced three- and four-story buildings.

Although most Kayenta cliff dwellings were considerably smaller than those in Mesa Verde, at least two were fairly large. Keet Seel, the largest cliff ruin in Arizona, had over 150 rooms, while Betatakin, contained almost as many. More than 50 of Betatakin's rooms were residential or living rooms, with 6 ceremonial rooms, 30 storage rooms, 2 grinding rooms, and 13 open patios or courts. Tree rings show that Betatakin was built and occupied between 1242 and 1277, Keet Seel from 1255 to 1286 A.D.

But perhaps the biggest difference between Kayenta and Mesa Verde cliff dwellings is in the kivas. Kayenta cliff dweller architects couldn't seem to agree on just how a kiva should be built. As a result they built two different kinds. One was the standard round subterranean kiva with ventilator, deflector, and fireplace but without pilasters. The other was a square or rectangular aboveground structure with the usual firepit and deflector, the latter facing toward a side door which served as the ventilating shaft.

Batwoman House, Betatakin, and Keet Seel, three contemporaneous Kayenta cliff dwellings, illustrate this diversity in kiva construction. At Batwoman House the Pueblo men built their kivas round and below ground. At Betatakin the men built their kivas square and above ground. The Keet Seel men, just to be contrary, built both square and round ceremonial rooms, above and below ground.

Perhaps we are doing the Kayenta architects an injustice. This change in kiva construction might well have been the result of the migration into the area of new peoples with new ideas on how ceremonial chambers should be built.

Rectangular ceremonial chambers were not new in the Southwest. At the Village of the Great Kivas, in addition to the small and large regular kivas, there were three rectangular rooms with such kiva-like features as deflector stones and ventilators. True rectangular kivas have also been uncovered in ruins over in eastern Arizona north of the Little Colorado River. Some of these pueblos, built in the late 1200's near the close of the Great Pueblo period, were quite large. These kivas had floors paved with sandstone slabs, firepits, deflectors, and ventilators. The ventilating shaft passed under a raised platform which formed an extension on the south side of the kiva, similar to the spectator bench in modern Hopi kivas.

The Pueblo building boom of the eleventh, twelfth, and thirteenth centuries came to a close near the end of the thirteenth century. After 1300 A.D. the Four Corners country was deserted.

# 10
# Pueblo Arts
# and Industries

Living in big towns had its advantages and its disadvantages. When hundreds of people began gathering together in pueblos of several stories, social, political, and religious life became more complicated. Individuals and groups had to learn how to live together and how to cooperate with each other in getting things done.

Probably about this time arose the feeling or idea expressed by our phrase "keeping up with the Joneses." With us this usually results in the acquiring of new drapes or a new stove or refrigerator or some other item of household equipment. However, a Pueblo family of the twelfth century had no real household furnishings. Although their architecture had advanced tremendously, their furniture was still meager. About all the average home had was several rush or willow mats, a few tanned deerskins, a storage bin or two, and perhaps an occasional pole shelf or clothes rack. That was all. Even as late as the nineteenth century most Hopi and other Pueblo Indian homes still lacked tables and chairs and beds and other things that we consider necessities.

Fig. 44. Thirteenth century cotton blanket painted with black designs.

But if the Pueblo housewife couldn't ask for a new carpet or a new refrigerator, she could and probably did nag her spouse for a new turquoise pendant or shell bracelet "like the one so-and-so was wearing yesterday." Or she might ask why he didn't weave her one of those new decorated cotton robes, clinching her argument with the classic remark that "all the other women have them."

For the manufacturing of clothing and ornaments had become big business. Cotton cloth had increased in importance to the point where it was a major item of trade. Many of the northern pueblos and cliff dwellings, because of their high elevation and cooler climate, couldn't grow their own cotton and had to barter for cotton lint or already woven squares of cloth which they could cut to suit their own taste. Spanish accounts of the sixteenth century show that the Hopi Indians of Arizona were growing large amounts of cotton and trading woven fabrics as far away as the Rio Grande pueblos in New Mexico.

More and better clothing seems to have been worn now. This may have been due to the greater abundance of fine cotton cloth. Or it may have been mere vanity or trying to keep up with the Joneses. Considering that they lacked scissors and buttons and zippers, these Pueblo peoples did very well for themselves.

Cotton was woven into squares or rectangles of cloth which were used as wrap-around loincloths or aprons, fastened at the waist by sashes. Larger pieces were sometimes used as ponchos by stitching together two corners and leaving a slit for the head. Women may have worn cotton robes as dresses, as some modern Pueblo women do, by wrapping them around the body under the left arm and fastening

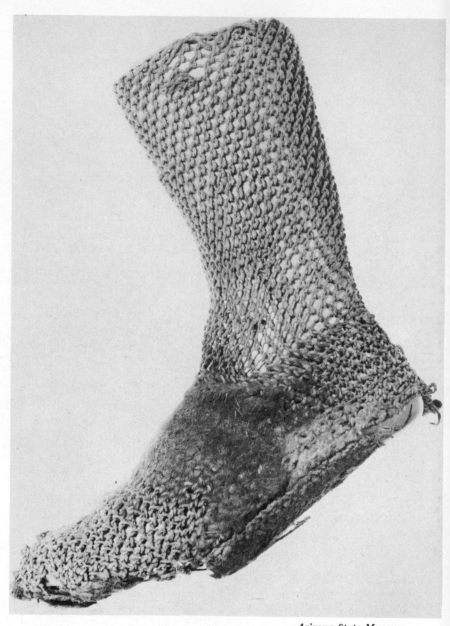

Fig. 45. Slipper sock of cotton thread reinforced with fur strips.

them over the right shoulder. Belts, sashes, arm bands, and blankets were also woven of cotton.

Many of these articles of cotton clothing were decorated in color — red, yellow, orange, blue, green, black, brown, and white. Sometimes the threads were dyed before they were woven into cloth; sometimes the finished cloth was painted with geometric designs. Variations in weaving techniques also produced such decorations as openwork patterns and diagonal or herringbone weaves. From a northern Arizona cliff dwelling came one unusual cotton specimen. This was a sandal sock or slipper sock made of cotton thread with a looping technique and reinforced with strips of fur.

Although cotton was seemingly abundant in many pueblos, particularly in those where it was grown, it was probably scarce and highly prized in others. Pieces of cotton cloth found in some cliff dwellings had been patched and mended and repatched and still worn long after they should have been thrown away.

Cotton might even be called a luxury cloth, perhaps the silk or mink of the thirteenth century. For those who couldn't afford cotton, there was always feather cloth, which furnished robes and blankets for the living and shrouds for the dead. One feather-cloth blanket from Pueblo Bonito measured 4 feet 3 inches by 6 feet 7 inches. Flocks of domestic turkeys were still kept for their feathers in many pueblos and cliff dwellings.

If even feather cloth was too expensive, there were still rabbit-fur blankets and robes of tanned deerskins and other animal hides. The long-time favorite fibers, yucca and Indian hemp, were still woven into bands and aprons, often decorated in color.

In fact, yucca probably still held its place as the most widely used plant material. Yucca leaves and fiber, as well as its roots and spiny tips, were turned into string and cord of all kinds, nets, snares, needles and sewing thread, brooms, soap for washing hair, hairbrushes, aprons, sandals, headbands, and mats.

Sandals continued in fashion as the standard footgear. There were a number of different types. Some sandals were round-toed, woven of yucca cord like those of the early Pueblo peoples. Others were coarsely woven of yucca leaves, either whole or split, with squarish toes. Still others were finely woven of Indian hemp or yucca fiber. These were similar in many ways to the finely woven sandals of the late Basketmakers. That is, they had raised decorations on the soles and quite often colored designs on the upper or lower surfaces or both. But the Pueblo weavers introduced a new wrinkle. Instead of notching the toes, they shaped them to fit the right or left foot. Sometimes they even made a jog for the little toe. Like earlier sandals, these were fastened on the foot by heel and toe loops or by side-loop ties.

Just as cotton was the luxury material for clothing, so turquoise was the favorite ornament among most Pueblo peoples. To the Pueblo Indian, turquoise was a gift from the gods. It may have been a gift, but it was certainly not free. It had to be dug out of the ground. Nearly every known turquoise outcrop in the Southwest has its deep pits strewn with stone hammers and other signs of prehistoric mining operations. The most famous of these mines are those of Los Cerillos, 25 miles southwest of Santa Fe, New Mexico. Here Pueblo miners had dug a number of pits, one of which was over 100 feet deep and 200 feet in diameter.

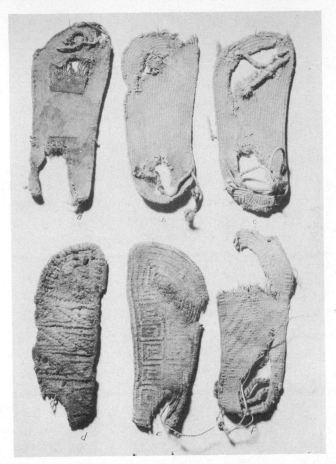

Fig. 46. Finely woven Pueblo sandals from cliff dwellings in northeastern Arizona.

These mines are believed to have supplied a large part of the turquoise so widely traded throughout the Southwest.

Turquoise furnished the material for the finest Pueblo ornaments — bead necklaces and bracelets, ear bobs, pendants, and mosaic inlays.

Pueblo Bonito seems to have led the way in the manufacture of turquoise jewelry. In one floor cache archaeologists uncovered two pairs of turquoise ear bobs and a 14-inch, four-strand necklace of 2,500 turquoise beads. With two burials in another room were nearly 15,000 turquoise beads and pendants. Everywhere the excavators dug they found still more turquoise beads and pendants and ear drops.

The Pueblo Indians also inlaid shell, basketry, and wood with bits of turquoise and other stones. At Aztec 20 inlaid shell disks were found lying on the chest of a skeleton. At Pueblo Bonito a walnut shell had been inlaid with turquoise and made into a pendant. A turquoise mosaic pendant of 17 oblong pieces of turquoise set in gum on a perforated wooden plate was found with one Kayenta burial.

The Bonitians even inlaid such utilitarian implements as deer bone scrapers with bands of turquoise and shell. At Poncho House cliff dwelling in southern Utah a flint blade 4½ inches long had been covered with turquoise, shell, and lignite in geometric patterns. Such an object, like the inlaid deer bone scrapers, was probably associated with some ceremony.

Making beads and pendants doesn't sound like much of a job. With only the crudest of stone tools, it took time and patience and plenty of elbow grease. Turquoise, for example, is harder than glass. Using sandstone saws and sandstone rubbing stones, the Indians cut and ground turquoise and other stones and shell. With sand as an abrasive, they bored larger holes with flint drills, smaller holes with cactus-tipped drills.

Stone beads were common in many areas. Two burials in a pueblo cemetery in the Kayenta area yielded a bracelet and a necklace of red and black stone beads strung on fine cord with occasional turquoise beads. Together the two strands represented about 100,000 individual beads.

Shells were also highly prized by the Pueblo Indians. In

most pueblos shell ornaments were even more abundant than those of turquoise. Traders must have been kept on the go twelve months of the year supplying the Pueblo Indians with shells from the Gulf of California and the Pacific Coast. Olivella, abalone, glycymeris, and conus were the most commonly used shells.

Shells were softer than turquoise and thus were easier to cut and make into beads, bracelets, and pendants. Shell pendants have been found carved in the shape of birds and animals and various geometric designs. Bracelets cut from large glycymeris shells were widely used.

Lignite or jet, sometimes called black turquoise by the Zuñi Indians, was popular with the occupants of Pueblo Bonito. Highly polished, it was carved into pendants and finger rings. Rings were also made of polished pieces of animal bones.

On ceremonial occasions, and probably on others also, Pueblo men and women supplemented their standard ornaments with a liberal application of face and body paint. Red was a favorite color in prehistoric times, as it still is today among the Pueblos, for marking the cheeks and forehead. Hematite or any other iron mineral that gave a reddish color was greatly valued. Certain iron oxides furnished yellow and brown paint, copper minerals green and blue, and gypsum white.

Kitchenware also reached a peak during this Classic period, not only in numbers of pots and pans made but also in variety and beauty of vessel shapes and designs. Although no two pots were ever decorated exactly alike, certain styles or patterns were the fashion in each area. These styles of design never remained in vogue for too long a time. Like our present-day fads in china, every 25 or 50 years or so saw the old style thrown on the dump heap and a new pattern taking its place.

The archaeologist who has handled thousands of pieces of Pueblo pottery can tell at a glance when and where a pot was manufactured. He would readily identify the black-on-white decorated bowl illustrated as having been made by a Kayenta Pueblo woman, probably some time between 1250 and 1280 A.D. The heavy use of black paint, producing what looks like a white design on a black background, is one of the distinguishing features of Kayenta black-on-white pottery.

Chaco Canyon black-on-white pottery is noted for its thinness and for its so-called hachured patterns, narrow black parallel lines filling in larger designs which were framed by heavier black lines. Up in Mesa Verde the Pueblo people manufactured their own distinctive black-on-white pots. These are generally fairly thick-walled, with

Fig. 47. Kayenta black-on-white bowl.

larger and more solid designs and square flat rims decorated with black dots.

Bowls, jars, and ladles were the common forms in all three areas. But each also had its own special vessel shapes. Kayenta potters made colanders, seed jars, and small jugs with handles. Mesa Verde women turned out quantities of flat-bottomed mugs and kiva jars, the latter having fitted covers. Chaco Canyon potters specialized in pitchers, tall cylindrical vases, and bird-shaped bowls and pitchers.

Although black-on-white was the characteristic decorated pottery during the Great Pueblo period, other colors were also used. Black-on-red pots were made throughout eastern and northeastern Arizona. Many of the Kayenta potters even produced polychrome (many-colored) pots, pottery decorated with more than two colors. On an orange background they painted designs in broad red lines outlined with black. Later they added a white outline.

Gray or grayish-black corrugated jars continued to be made and used as cooking vessels. Although they were better made in some areas than in others, they do not show the variations of painted pottery. Many had geometric patterns formed by indenting the corrugated coils with the fingernail or a pointed stick. These cooking jars ranged from small to large, all with wide mouths.

When a pot broke, that wasn't the end of its usefulness. Larger pieces could be used as scrapers. Smaller fragments could be worked into circular disks to serve as gaming counters or, perforated, as spindle whorls. Sometimes a brightly decorated piece would be worn suspended around the neck as a pendant. Still smaller chunks were ground up and used as tempering material for the next batch of pots.

If a favorite pot was merely cracked, however, it was

Fig. 48. Pueblo flat-type metates and manos.

generally mended. Small holes were bored with a flint drill on either side of the crack and fiber cord or sinew laced tightly across the break. Sometimes the crack was also sealed with pitch.

The Pueblo Indians were a Stone Age people. For most of their household tools and implements they used the only materials they had available — stone, bone, and wood.

Stone was pecked or ground into metates and manos, mortars and pestles, hammers, mauls, axes, picks, hoes, scrapers, jar covers, arrow-shaft polishers, rubbing stones, polishing stones, knives, drills, chisels, spearheads, and arrowheads. Some of these remained the simple tools their fathers and grandfathers had used for centuries. Others, however, changed during the Great Pueblo period.

A radical change, for example, took place in Pueblo corn grinding tools. In earlier times metates had been trough-shaped, portable, grooved slabs of rock that could be moved from place to place as needed. But now flat or slightly concave metates, with all-over grinding surfaces, began to be used. Since there were no borders to keep meal from spilling over the edges, these new metates were set permanently in bins.

This new house fixture was generally located near the corner of a room. A metate was imbedded in hard-packed clay, tilted forward at an angle of 20 to 30 degrees, and walled in with flat sandstone slabs set on edge in the floor. Under the lower end of the metate was a hollow where a basket or bowl could be placed to catch the ground meal. Occasionally this hollow was also paved with sandstone slabs.

Sometimes only a single metate was put in such a bin, but usually they were in groups of two or three, each of a different type of rock. The first, or coarsest, would be of lava, the second of sandstone, and the third of fine-grained sandstone or granite. With two or three or more metates women could grind their cornmeal to whatever degree of fineness they desired.

The manos or hand stones used to grind the corn also

Fig. 49. Flat metates in walled-in mealing bin.

changed. They became longer, from 12 to 18 inches in length, long enough to reach clear across the metates. Their undersides were slightly convex to fit the concave surfaces of the metates. Sometimes small grooves were pecked in the front and back sides as thumb and finger grips. Manos were made of lava or sandstone, lava manos being used on lava metates, sandstone manos on sandstone metates. Judging from the great numbers of manos uncovered, every Pueblo housewife must have kept a liberal supply on hand.

When the grinding surface on a metate became too smooth to grind cornmeal properly, it had to be pecked and roughened. As it was, an unbelievable amount of sand must have been ground into the meal. This is reflected in the well-worn teeth found in most Pueblo Indian jaws.

The flat metate and mealing bin complex seems to have been too revolutionary a change for some Pueblo people to accept. Flat metates made their appearance just before the opening of the Great Pueblo period, but it was several centuries before they were universally adopted. At Pueblo Bonito only grooved metates were used, and in only two of the hundreds of rooms were there mealing bins. Pueblo del Arroyo inhabitants were also conservatives. Mealing bins were found in only three rooms, and in only one of these was there a flat metate. Yet only 75 miles to the southwest the last occupants of the Village of the Great Kivas had discarded grooved metates and were using flat metates in mealing bins.

Still another change came in stone axes. Up to this time all Pueblo axes had been full-grooved. But now trade with the Hohokam people in southern Arizona began to bring in a new type of ax. This had the groove extending only three-quarters of the way around the ax head. Both types of axes

Fig. 50. Full-grooved Pueblo stone axes.

Fig. 51. Three-quarter-grooved Hohokam-type stone axes.

were generally made of diorite, but the full-grooved axes were usually shorter, stubbier, and often not as well smoothed and polished.

Most Pueblo Indians didn't take to this new style in axes. One reason may have been because it meant a change in the method of hafting. At the Village of the Great Kivas the majority of the people continued to make and use full-grooved axes. Chaco Canyon residents were even more reluctant to change. Three or four three-quarter-grooved axes found their way to Pueblo Bonito and Pueblo del Arroyo. But their new owners quickly pecked out the backs and converted them into full-grooved axes.

A few axes were double-bitted. It is thought that these may have been war axes as they were lighter in weight and better balanced.

Although axes were mainly used for cutting and shaping wood, they were probably handy tools to have around the house. The battered butt ends of most axes indicate that they were frequently used as hammers.

Axes were also valued articles of trade. Back in the nineteenth century an old Navaho told a United States Army captain that a stone ax would formerly buy a wife. While we don't say that this custom was followed among the Pueblos, it does show that stone axes were possessions highly regarded by most southwestern Indians.

Other stone tools that changed during the Great Pueblo period were the so-called arrow shaft polishers or straighteners. These grooved stones are thought to have been used in smoothing, shaping, and rounding arrow shafts, spindle shafts, and similar wooden objects. Simple stones with one or two grooves had been known and used for some time. By the twelfth and thirteenth centuries the Pueblo

Fig. 52. Stone arrow shaft polishers.

Indians were taking more pride in their work and were making better-finished arrow shaft polishers.

The Pueblo Indians seem to have spent a lot of time smoothing and polishing implements. When an Indian had an ax to sharpen, he rubbed it up and down on the first sandstone surface he could find. This might be the cliff in back of the pueblo or the doorstep into his living room. Well-worn grooves in sandstone boulders and cliffs show where bone awls and needles were pointed and sharpened in the same way.

Nearly every prehistoric pueblo ruin has its share of objects which seem to have served no practical purpose. Archaeologists generally lump all such strange or unusual items into a ceremonial grab bag.

Ceremony of one kind or another lay at the heart of Pueblo society. The Pueblo Indian took his religion seriously, seven days a week. He believed that supernatural beings, spirits, controlled the elements and all objects. To gain their influence gifts had to be given and ceremonies performed. Songs, dances, prayers, ritual smoking, offerings, all played their part in Pueblo Indian religion.

For these the Indians used prayer sticks, feathers, tobacco pipes, fossil shells, quartz crystals, sacred cornmeal, carved figurines, painted wooden altars, painted wood, bone, and stone objects, decorated baskets, medicine bags, bone whistles, wooden flutes, deer hoof rattles, and ceremonial costumes. All these have been found in pueblo ruins.

Prayer sticks, thought of as messengers carrying prayers to the gods, were used by the thousands, each ritual requiring its special prayer stick. Willow and other woods were easy to get, but feathers, a necessary part of nearly every prayer stick, presented a more difficult problem. Turkeys, both domestic and wild, red-tailed hawks, eagles, owls, and other birds furnished many of the feathers needed. But seemingly they were not enough.

To meet the demand parrot and macaw feathers were imported from northern Mexico. These brilliant green, red, blue, and yellow feathers soon became so popular that live birds were brought in across the thousand miles of deserts and mountains. In exchange the traders took back turquoise. One dark storage room at Pueblo Bonito had even been converted into a cage for macaws. A 40-in-wide, adobe-covered shelf had been built across one end of the small room. Then, some time later, the ceiling had fallen in and buried the room. When archaeologists finally dug down into it, they found macaw debris on the shelf and floor. Beneath the remains of the shelf and ceiling they discovered the skeletons of four macaws and the skull of a fifth. That these birds were transported alive is shown by the numerous skeletons of parrots and macaws found in Pueblo Bonito and other villages. Macaw feathers are still in demand today by the Macaw clan at Zuñi.

Small copper bells were also traded northward from Mexico, reaching Pueblo Bonito and some other settlements. These may have been used either as ornaments or as ritual objects.

Ritual smoking begins and ends most Pueblo Indian ceremonies, the smoke clouds being thought of as symbolic of rain clouds. Probably the same beliefs were held by their ancestors during the Great Pueblo period. In addition to tubular clay and stone pipes or cloud blowers, elbow pipes similar to pipes of today also began to be manufactured.

A mystery surrounds the burials of this Classic period. Although the cemeteries of the smaller villages have been found in the adjacent rubbish heaps, the burial grounds of the larger pueblos and cliff dwellings have never been located.

In Chaco Canyon, in Mesa Verde, in Kayenta, the story is the same. Here and there a few burials have been uncovered — an occasional isolated skeleton buried in a trash mound, a few infants put beneath house floors, half a dozen adults laid away in abandoned storage rooms. That is all. Search as hard as they might, archaeologists haven't been able to find the real graveyards.

During Pueblo Bonito's 200-year-long occupation, archaeologists estimate that approximately 5,000 Bonitians

Fig. 53. Extended Pueblo burial with pottery bowl as grave offering.

must have died and, presumably, been buried near by. Yet less than 100 skeletons have been found, and those were all within the pueblo. What became of the other 4,900 is still an unsolved puzzle.

Some have tried to explain the mystery by suggesting that the Pueblo Indians, like the Hohokam, cremated their dead. But even cremation would leave behind many burned areas and fragments of partly burned bones. None of these have ever been found. Actually, the Anasazi rarely, if ever, practiced cremation.

Most Pueblo Indian skeletons that have been dug up were buried in rubbish heaps, in trash-filled corners of caves, in courtyards, or in abandoned rooms in houses. The majority of bodies were laid away in a flexed or partially flexed position, just as in earlier periods. But in some pueblos, particularly during the latter part of the era, many bodies were stretched out flat on the back, full length. At Pueblo Bonito the early burials were flexed or partially flexed, the later ones extended full length.

Another burial practice now adopted in some areas was that of orienting the bodies. Although there was apparently no fixed rule, many bodies were placed with the heads to the east, facing west. At the Village of the Great Kivas, out of 60 burials uncovered in refuse mounds, 46 had the head placed more or less toward the east. Most Pueblo Bonito burials also had their heads to the east.

From the handful of Pueblo burials that have been found we know that bodies were customarily wrapped in feather robes or cotton blankets and laid on mats of willows or bulrushes. Occasionally a wooden pillow was put under the head of a burial. With the bodies were left offerings of pottery, basketry, implements, clothing, and ornaments. Sometimes the grave was covered with sandstone slabs or with logs.

Grave robbing seems to have been a profitable business back in the twelfth century. Out of 68 burials made in abandoned storage rooms in Pueblo Bonito, 46 had been dragged from their graves and relieved of their jewelry. The few undisturbed burials indicate that the dead were well equipped with ornaments for their journey into the afterworld. One female lying on a bulrush mat had a turquoise pendant on her chest and a turquoise bead bracelet on her left wrist. Grouped about her head and shoulders were fourteen pottery vessels and an oval basket tray.

In another room at Pueblo Bonito archaeologists discovered where twelve bodies had been buried in the trash covering the floor. Unfortunately grave robbers had found them nearly 800 years before. All twelve bodies had been ripped from their graves and searched for valuables. We don't know just how much the thieves got, but in their haste they missed hundreds of turquoise beads and pendants which the later excavators recovered. The robbers also left 27 pots, 22 ceremonial staffs, and 8 wooden flageolets, probably because these were too bulky to cart off.

But the archaeologists were lucky at that. The grave robbers hadn't dug quite deep enough. Beneath the floor the twentieth-century diggers discovered two additional bodies lying full length in carefully prepared burial vaults, still with all their jewelry intact. With one skeleton were ten turquoise pendants and 5,980 beads. With the other were 698 pendants, over 9,000 turquoise beads, and numerous inlaid baskets, shell ornaments, and other offerings.

Because of the small size of the rooms and doorways in most cliff dwellings and pueblos many people think that the

Indians must have been midgets. They were not. Nor were they giants as others believe. The Pueblo Indians were just averaged-sized. Of all the hundreds of skeletons measured, the shortest was a female 4 feet 6 inches tall, the tallest a male 5 feet 8 inches in height. Most ranged between 5 feet and 5 feet 6 inches.

These Indians suffered from many of the same ailments and diseases that afflict us today. An occasional middle-aged individual shows traces of arthritis or rheumatism. A number show spinal and other bone deformities that probably resulted from malnutrition and vitamin deficiency. Others had broken arms and legs. And a few others met violent deaths, either by blows on the head from the proverbial blunt instrument or by arrows through the body.

Perhaps the most apparent ailment in Pueblo days was bad teeth. Pyorrhea was common. Cavities were numerous. Nearly every skull of a middle-aged person had one or more missing molars, and some elderly individuals had lost all their teeth. An aching tooth was probably removed with a sharp pointed stick. But once teeth were out, they couldn't be replaced. There were no false teeth in the Southwest during the Great Pueblo period.

Hard cradle boards were still the fashion. Nearly every skull showed the characteristic flattening at the back of the head.

All these studies show that the Pueblo Indians of the eleventh, twelfth, and thirteenth centuries were not much different physically from their descendants of the twentieth century.

# 11
# Abandonment of the Four Corners

The story of the Pueblo Indians in the Four Corners country comes to an end about 1300 A.D. People had begun leaving the area as early as the latter part of the twelfth century and had kept on moving out for the next hundred years. Those who stayed behind gathered into large pueblos and cliff dwellings. Then, shortly before the close of the thirteenth century, the last of the cliff dwellers pulled up stakes and headed for points south and east.

From that time on the only signs of Pueblo peoples in this northern region were occasional roving hunting parties from the southern towns.

Why the people left is not an easy question to answer. Causes and reasons for events that happened nearly 700 years ago can't be dug up like burials and pots.

Because archaeologists couldn't at first give a definite explanation for the abandonment of the Four Corners country, all sorts of wild theories were proposed. In these theories the causes ranged from epidemic diseases that wiped out the entire population to hordes of fierce nomadic tribes

167

who poured in from the north, killing off most of the Cliff Dwellers and forcing the survivors to flee for their lives.

Neither of these theories seemed likely. There was no evidence of pestilence or of slaughter at the hands of invading tribes. Yet the building of watchtowers and the concentration into large pueblos and cliff dwellings did seem to indicate defensive measures against somebody. But against whom?

We know the Apaches and Navahos were in the Southwest by the 1500's and were even then raiding the Pueblo Indians. But we can't prove they were there 300 years earlier. Nor do we know how long the Utes and Paiutes and other nomadic tribes have been in Utah and Colorado. Even if some of these had been there that early, they were probably not as numerous as the Pueblo Indians. The country could not have supported large numbers of people living entirely off wild plants and animals. It doesn't seem possible that small, widely scattered bands of nomads, on foot and armed only with spears and bows and arrows, could have caused enough trouble to force the Cliff Dwellers to abandon their homeland. Further, there is little actual evidence of warfare during this period.

But the archaeologists couldn't come up with any better answers until they received help from geologists and an astronomer. The astronomer was, of course, Dr. Douglass, the discoverer of tree ring dating. His studies showed that the Southwest had suffered an extremely severe drought lasting from 1276 to 1299 A.D. During that quarter of a century comparatively little rain fell.

Now these prehistoric Pueblo Indians were, first and foremost, farmers. Their living depended upon the plants they cultivated — corn, beans, squash, and cotton. Their farms were seldom large. An acre or two here, three or four there, they dotted the mesa tops and the canyon bottoms about their villages. They depended upon winter rainfall and snowfall stored in the ground to start their plants in the spring, and late summer rains to finish the job.

Unlike their southern neighbors, the Hohokam, they didn't have permanent streams of water in which they could build irrigation dams and extensive canal systems. Their water supply was limited. In some areas they did put up small check dams which captured water from summer rains and spread it over their fields.

The greatest disaster that could happen to a bunch of farmers would be a drought. The droughts that hit many of our plains states in the 1930's and again in the 1950's are vivid examples.

Further, this prehistoric drought, from 1276 to 1299 A.D., fits in very well with some tree ring dates from Mesa Verde and Kayenta pueblos and cliff dwellings. Tree rings tell us that all building came to an end in the Four Corners country during this same period. At Square Tower House the last beam was put up in 1259, at Cliff Palace in 1273, at Square Tower House in 1274, at Batwoman House in 1275, at Betatakin and Long House in 1277, at Scaffold House in 1278, and at Balcony House in 1279. Seven years later, in 1286, the final post was set up at Keet Seel. After that date we can find no record of building or remodeling going on anywhere in this northern region.

To some archaeologists this great drought explains everything. But others raise a few objections. The drought, while long, was probably not much more severe than others the Indians had lived through in preceding centuries. In fact, the Southwest had been going through a dry period since the early 1200's. Nor were all the large pueblos and cliff dwellings abandoned at the same time, as they likely would have been if the drought had been the sole cause. Clans and bands had been moving away from the Mesa Verde and Kayenta villages for well over a hundred years before the drought. Some towns were deserted long before 1276 while others continued to be inhabited for ten or more years after the dry spell began.

All this seems to indicate that the drought was not the only cause. Something else must also have been at work. Recently geologists have discovered what may be the answer. This is arroyo cutting. An arroyo is a deep gully or channel cut into a canyon bottom. During years when rainfall is low, although not necessarily low enough to be called a drought, arroyos begin to form at the lower end of valleys and gradually extend their way back toward the headwaters.

The Pueblo Indians were flood-water farmers, depending upon floods spreading out over the canyon floors to water their crops. But when arroyo cutting began, these plains not only were cut by deep gullies but the water table was also lowered so much that the fields became useless. This was a slow process. At first only the lower fields were lost. The next year or the following year perhaps a few more were washed away. In time the entire canyon might be made unusable.

Segie Canyon illustrates this process. In the twelfth and thirteenth centuries it was the home of hundreds of Pueblo Indians living in Betatakin and Keet Seel and other cliff dwellings. Then a cycle of arroyo cutting began and washed away their farm lands. The Pueblo Indians left and never came back. Centuries later the cycle changed and silt and sand drifted in, filling up the arroyos. In the nine-teenth century groups of Navaho Indians raised corn in the canyon and herded bands of sheep and horses. But in 1884 a new cycle of erosion came along and the present deep arroyos were cut. Now only a handful of Navahos inhabit Segie Canyon.

Arroyo cutting hits at the heart of a farmer's life, his land; a drought at his water supply. A combination of these two factors, perhaps coupled with occasional raids by no-madic hunting tribes, would seem to be the correct answer as to why the Four Corners country was abandoned.

Arroyo cutting, together with nomadic raids, would ex-plain why some groups began leaving as early as the twelfth century. With more and more land being lost by arroyo cutting and with increased pressure from hostile nomads, a severe drought would be the final blow. With most of their farm lands gone, with their water low, the Pueblo In-dians up and left in search of better country where they could live in peace.

The Cliff Dwellers didn't disappear into thin air as some people think. We know where many of them went. Since the ninth and tenth centuries the Anasazi had been expand-ing and spreading out north, south, east, and west. For per-haps the first time in their nearly thousand-year history they were giving more than they were receiving.

They had established outposts far up the Colorado River in eastern Utah and western Colorado, reaching nearly to the Wyoming border. Here they introduced agriculture, pottery, clay figurines, rock paintings and carvings, pit-houses, and, later, masonry houses. But most of this northern area had been abandoned by the time the Great Pueblo period got under way in the Four Corners country.

Other groups of early migrants had wandered west to establish villages along the Grand Canyon. Some had even reached southwestern Utah and southeastern Nevada where they built hundreds of pueblos and some cliff dwellings. But the drought eventually caught up with them and caused them to return to Arizona.

Other groups had gone south to join neighboring tribes in the vicinity of Flagstaff, Arizona. These local Indians, called Sinagua by archaeologists, lived in deep pithouses with long side entrances and made brown pottery similar to that of the Mogollon people. The Sinagua Indians dwelt peacefully in their small villages until the year 1064 A.D. Somewhere between September 1064 and June 1065, according to the detective work of tree ring experts, the Sinagua people were startled to find a volcano erupting in their front yards.

This volcano, now known as Sunset Crater, buried the villages under a cloud of volcanic cinders and ashes. The frightened Indians took to their heels. But when a few venturesome individuals discovered that the blanket of cinders absorbed moisture and grew fine crops of corn and beans, the land boom was on.

Anasazi Indians from northern Arizona poured in to the 800 square miles of cinder-covered land. So did Hohokam bands from the south and Mogollon peoples from the southeast. At first each group maintained its separate identity. But before long Anasazi architecture was adopted throughout the region. Hundreds of pueblos were built, including such two- and three-story structures as Wukoki, Wupatki, Citadel, Turkey Hill Pueblo, and Elden Pueblo.

Wupatki, a Hopi word meaning "tall house," was the largest pueblo in the cinder zone. Three stories high in

*—National Park Service*

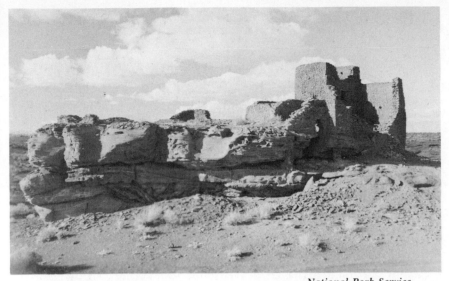

Fig. 54. Wukoki Ruin in Wupatki National Monument, Arizona.

Fig. 55. Small cliff dwellings in Walnut Canyon National Monument, Arizona.

*—National Park Service*

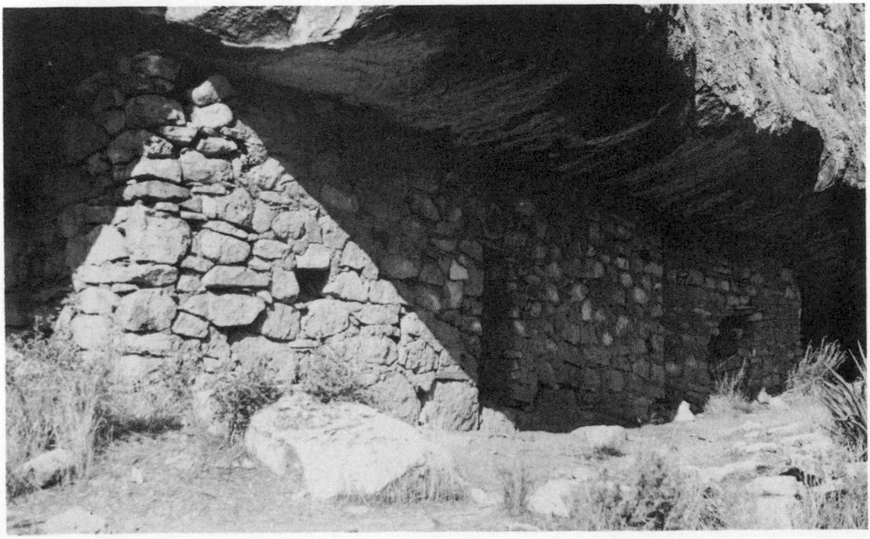

places, it contained over a hundred rooms and an unroofed circular ceremonial court 50 feet in diameter. A few hundred feet away was a masonry ball court, showing that Hohokam influence was also strong.

Wupatki, with a population of 200 to 300, must have been the ceremonial and trading center of the region. Black-on-white pottery flooded in from northeastern and eastern Arizona. Shell came in from the Pacific Coast and the Gulf of California, turquoise from the east. Even traders bringing colorful macaws made the long journey up from Mexico.

The Sinagua Indians, probably through knowledge acquired from the Anasazi, also began constructing cliff dwellings. At Walnut Canyon, a few miles southeast of Flagstaff, are the remains of more than 300 cliff houses. These were all small, one- and two-room structures built on narrow ledges and using the overhanging roof for ceilings.

These mixed peoples weren't poor country cousins, outcasts from the larger and richer northern and southern cultures. From Ridge Ruin, a small pueblo of some 20 to 25 rooms located 20 miles east of Flagstaff, came one of the richest burials ever found in the Southwest. Archaeologists from the Museum of Northern Arizona dug into a semi-subterranean masonry room and discovered the stretched-out body of what must have been a medicine man. With him were 613 different offerings, including 25 pots, 8 baskets, one of which was a tube covered with a 1500-piece turquoise and stone mosaic, half a dozen elaborate turquoise and shell mosaic inlays, nearly 4,000 stone, turquoise, and shell beads and pendants, a dozen carved wooden ceremonial objects, several bone awls, 420 arrowheads, and a collection of paints and minerals.

But the land boom didn't last too long. Shortly after 1200

a dry period set in. Winds piled up the light cinders and ashes into drifts too deep to cultivate. Our last tree ring date is 1278, at Turkey Hill Pueblo, 12 miles east of Flagstaff. But long before then people had begun to leave. Some went east into the Little Colorado River valley. Others went south into the well-watered Verde valley. By 1300 A.D. the Flagstaff country was deserted.

But we are getting away from the story of what became of the Cliff Dwellers. Others from the Kayenta area went south 50 to 60 miles to the far end of Black Mesa and adjoining Antelope Mesa. This was a sandy, desert-like country, but the springs of water seeping out of the rocky cliffs looked good to the newcomers. They weren't the first to settle down around the springs. Earlier Anasazi, discovering that crops could be grown on the slopes where sand formed a mulch, had been living continuously in the area since Basketmaker times.

Still others seem to have gone on farther south into the Petrified Forest area and beyond into the forested mountains of eastern Arizona and western New Mexico. The Anasazi trait of building stone pueblos had preceded them, spreading rapidly all the way down to southern New Mexico. Mogollon pithouses were gradually replaced by masonry structures. Black-on-white pottery soon became the chief decorated type. In fact, some of the best black-on-white pots in the Southwest were made by these Anasazi-Mogollon people.

Down in southern New Mexico, one of these mixed groups, called Mimbres after a small river of that name, produced a unique style of black-on-white pottery. Many bowls were decorated with finely drawn geometric designs. But others had, in addition, realistic drawings of insects, birds, animals, and human beings. Some of these figures were fantastic combinations of human and animal creatures.

Another of these mixed Anasazi and Mogollon groups of the twelfth and thirteenth centuries was the Salado, so-called after the Rio Salado, the early Spanish name for the Salt River. Along about 1100 these Salado people had moved south and west from the upper Little Colorado area into the Tonto Basin below the Mogollon Rim. There they began building small one- and two-story houses of masonry and adobe clay inside compound walls. They added poly-chrome pots, black, white, and red, to their distinctive black-on-white and corrugated types.

In the thirteenth century refugees from the northern drought areas swarmed into the country below the Mogol-lon Rim and adopted Salado ways of life.

Many of the Salado pushed on still further south and west into the Gila River basin where they joined the Hohokam. These newcomers introduced their own styles of architec-ture, building thick-walled, multistoried community houses of adobe enclosed within massive compound walls. They also brought in polychrome pottery and burial of the dead.

So far as we can tell this was a peaceful invasion. The two peoples lived side by side in the same communities, with

Fig. 56. Mimbres black-on-white pottery from southern New Mexico.

each group retaining most of its own customs. The Hohokam, for example, continued to make their typical red-on-buff pottery and still cremated their dead.

But we are again wandering a long way from our northern Cliff Dwellers. Many former Mesa Verde residents made their way southeastward into the upper Rio Grande River valley where they joined other Anasazi groups who had preceded them. There they began building pueblos in the valleys and canyons and on the mesa tops.

By 1300 A.D. all of the Kayenta and Mesa Verde peoples had found new homes elsewhere in Arizona and New Mexico. The Four Corners country, which had been their homeland for well over a thousand years, was abandoned to the lizards and jackrabbits and buzzards.

# 12
# Pueblo
# Revival

The abandonment of the Four Corners country and the resettling of the Anasazi in other areas to the south and southeast marked the opening of a new era. Archaeologists had at first named this the Regressive period, believing that there had been a decline in architecture and in arts and industries. But the more sites they excavated, the more they were convinced that they had misnamed the period.

Actually there had been no decline. Once the Pueblo Indians got through shifting around and had time to become acquainted with their new homelands and new neighbors, they forged rapidly ahead. They built some of their largest pueblos during the fourteenth and fifteenth centuries. They also made some of their best pottery. Corrugated pots died out and black-on-white decorated ware practically disappeared, but they were never missed. Replacing them were elaborate painted types, particularly polychromes, in a wide range of styles. Designs frequently included birds, animals, insects, and human figures. Glaze paint also began to be used in many areas.

Archaeologists finally came to the conclusion that the

179

period might better be termed a renaissance or revival era, a second golden age.

New centers sprang up to take the place of Chaco, Mesa Verde, and Kayenta. The Hopi mesas in northern Arizona, the mountainous belt across central and eastern Arizona, the Zuñi country in western New Mexico, and the Rio Grande Valley all now rose to prominence. Just as in preceding periods, the peoples of each of these areas soon began to develop their own distinctive ways of making everything from houses to pots.

The Verde River valley southwest of Flagstaff, Arizona, was one of these new areas that experienced a sudden jump in population. Pueblo peoples from the north, as well as Sinagua and other groups, moved into the well-watered valley when the thirteenth-century drought hit. These refugees built new apartment houses and also added on to already established pueblos.

One of the largest of the latter was Tuzigoot, now preserved as a national monument. Originally Tuzigoot had been a small cluster of 15 or 20 rooms up on a hill beside the Verde River. By the end of the drought it had doubled and redoubled in population and size until it contained 110 rooms arranged in two groups with a plaza in between.

All up and down the valley were still other large pueblos. Some of the Anasazi newcomers even managed to find a few caves in the limestone cliffs and build cliff dwellings. Perhaps the most famous of these was Montezuma Castle, also now a national monument. Its discoverors, like those at Aztec Pueblo, confused its builders with the Aztecs of Mexico and one of their emperors. Perched high on a rocky ledge, Montezuma Castle was a five-story structure with 20 rooms. A hundred yards away was another five-story

Fig. 57. Montezuma Castle National Monument, Arizona.

cliff dwelling of 45 rooms. This building had collapsed in prehistoric times as a result of a fire in its upper rooms.

Seven miles northeast of Montezuma Castle lies Montezuma Well, a big limestone sink half filled with flowing water. Indians built small cliff dwellings and pueblos around the well, running the water through ditches to irrigate their farms.

For some reason the Indians at Montezuma Castle and most of the other cliff dwellings and pueblos in the Verde Valley never seem to have manufactured much decorated pottery of their own. They made a number of local varieties of plain browns and reds, but their painted pots they imported from the Pueblo people living to the north on Black Mesa and Antelope Mesa.

With the opening of the fourteenth century this northern

Arizona mesa country had really begun to boom. In addition to immigrants from the last of the Kayenta cliff dwellings, peoples from all over the surrounding countryside had poured into the area in a steady stream. Old pueblos were added on to and new and bigger ones were constructed.

From this time on we can call these people by the name by which we know their descendants today, the Hopi Indians. For the Hopi have never left their mesa homeland from that day to this. At least one of these old Hopi towns, Oraibi, has been continuously inhabited right on down to the present. Oraibi has, in fact, been called the oldest continuously occupied town in the United States. Tree rings tell us that others of these old Hopi villages date back to the fourteenth and fifteenth centuries.

Some of these early Hopi towns were big, covering from one to ten or twelve acres of ground. Often they consisted of rectangular blocks of one- to three-story houses built in rows along streets or around open courtyards. The Hopis returned to the practice of putting their kivas in the courtyards. But their kivas were rectangular, about 12 or 14 feet square, with a platform or bench at one end above the ventilating shaft. In each were the usual firepit, deflector, and sipapu. Floors were generally paved with flat sandstone slabs. Some of the finest mural decorations of the fourteenth and fifteenth centuries were painted on the walls of many of these Hopi kivas.

The Hopis became the first prehistoric peoples in North America to mine soft coal and use it to heat their houses. In rooms where coal was used small chimneys were built to carry off the fumes.

Out of this mixing of peoples in the Hopi country came a number of new pottery types. The old-style black-on-white painted pots gave way to a black-on-yellow ware which lasted practically unchanged for nearly 300 years. It was widely traded all over Arizona and New Mexico. Along in the fifteenth century the Hopis also began making beautiful polychrome vessels by painting designs in both black and red on the yellow background. During the next 200 years they manufactured some of the best pottery found anywhere in the Southwest.

Our scene now shifts 100 to 150 miles to the south. Shortly before 1300 A.D. refugees from the northern cliff dwellings, as well as from other drought-stricken areas, crowded into the uplands of eastern Arizona. These forested, well-watered mountains and valleys represented a different kind of country from what most of these northerners had been used to. But they quickly made themselves at home, either moving in with earlier residents or settling down in new towns of their own.

Like their Hopi cousins, these eastern Arizona peoples of the fourteenth century went in for big pueblos. The larger ones contained up to 800 rooms arranged in two- and three-story rectangular blocks, often with one or more plazas.

Kivas seem not to have been as plentiful in most pueblos as they were in the north. They were generally rectangular in shape, with a bench or alcove along the south side. Low

Fig. 58. Early Hopi black-on-yellow pottery.

benches encircling some courtyards indicate that these plazas may have served as ceremonial centers. One such rectangular courtyard even had a stone platform or altar on its southern side.

Some of these newcomers, perhaps former Cliff Dwellers, found caves in the canyon cliffs just west of the White Mountains and built cliff pueblos for themselves. Most of these were small, ranging from three to sixty rooms.

Like the Hopis, these mountain dwellers preferred polychrome pottery. But their decorated pots were painted black, white, and red in a variety of combinations and styles. They also imported pots from the Hopi country and from other neighboring areas. From the quantities of foreign pots found in some of the pueblos, these may have been trading centers.

One of the largest of these pueblos was Kinishba, located just west of Whiteriver on what is now the Fort Apache Indian Reservation. Kinishba, an Apache Indian word meaning "brown house," was excavated by a team from the University of Arizona. It was made up of two rectangular groups of two- and three-story rooms separated by a shallow wash which probably formerly held a spring. The smaller block contained at least 210 ground-floor rooms surrounding a large patio.

Until the latter part of the thirteenth century Kinishba had been a small pueblo of less than a hundred rooms. But within the next twenty-five years it had quadrupled in size to become one of the largest and richest towns in the region. Thousands of pieces of pottery, metates and manos, stone axes, arrow shaft polishers, and other implements and utensils were found in the rooms. Ornaments were particularly numerous. In a cache in one room were 1140 gypsum pen-

Fig. 59. An excavated room in Kinishba Pueblo in eastern Arizona.

dants. In another room was a clam shell inlaid with 367 small pieces of turquoise, with a rectangular piece of red shell in the center. Ceremonial objects were also abundant, including oval and rectangular stones painted in red, orange, black, yellow, and white; painted deer bones, quartz crystals, perforated bear claws, and stone pipes.

Hohokam influence was shown in the stone axes, most of those recovered being of the three-quarter-grooved type. Hohokam influence also appeared in methods of burial. Out of over a hundred skeletons found, three were cremations. The rest of the dead had been buried in the refuse mounds or in abandoned rooms. Only five bodies were fully flexed. Most were stretched out flat on the back, with the head commonly to the east.

Showlow, another large late pueblo north of Kinishba, is famous as the site of HH-39, the charcoal beam that proved to be the key to the dating of prehistoric ruins by tree rings.

Fig. 60. Pueblo burial at Kinishba.

At Kinishba, as at most of the other mountain pueblos, the invasion of new peoples in the late 1200's was a peaceful one. The newcomers may not exactly have been welcomed with open arms, but they settled down alongside the old-timers without any outward fuss. Yet this wasn't always the case. In at least one instance the new peoples seem to have worn out their welcome within a very few years.

This was at Point of Pines Pueblo south of Kinishba on the present San Carlos Apache Indian Reservation. Excavated by the University of Arizona, Point of Pines formed a solid block of over 800 rooms, most of which had been constructed after 1300. In the late 1200's the pueblo consisted of some 70 rooms in an L-shaped, two-story structure. Near by was another, similar pueblo. Upon excavation, it was discovered that the 70-room pueblo had been built about 1280 by a group of fifty to sixty families who had migrated south from the Kayenta region. They brought with them their own architecture and pots and corn and ceremonies and kept on making and doing things as they had up north. Maybe they looked down their noses at their neighbors and their ways of life. We don't know. We do know that shortly after 1300 the native residents rose up and burned at least eighteen rooms in the pueblo, mainly rooms jammed full of corn and other newly harvested crops. The newcomers took the hint and left. The only indication of their former presence was a defensive wall the old-timers soon built around the town.

This may have been a unique case, or something similar may have happened fairly frequently. Not enough of these late sites have been excavated to give us the answer.

But the building boom in the Verde Valley and Tonto Basin and White Mountains didn't last too long. By 1350 many of the smaller cliff dwellings and pueblos had been abandoned. By 1400 the residents of most of the larger ones had also departed. About this same time the Salado people who had moved in with the Hohokam also pulled out.

Not too long after the fifteenth century opened, then, Point of Pines, Kinishba, Grasshopper, Showlow, Fourmile, Gila Pueblo, Montezuma Castle, Tuzigoot, and all the other cliff dwellings and pueblos in this southern desert and mountain land were deserted.

And once again we don't know exactly why this exodus took place. We can't blame it on another drought. Arroyo cutting might have been responsible for the loss of needed farm lands. Perhaps there were internal troubles such as disputes between factions or between villages. Or, as some archaeologists believe, incoming nomadic bands of Apache Indians may have begun raiding the fields and towns.

Whatever the reason or reasons, the Pueblo Indians did leave. Some of them went north to the Hopi country. Certain modern Hopi clans have traditions that tell how their ancestors came from the Verde Valley and central Arizona. Others seem to have gone northeast into western New Mexico, to the country just south of the present town of Gallup, New Mexico.

This region is now the Zuñi Indian Reservation. There, today's Zuñi Pueblo Indians got their start nearly a thousand years ago. Traditionally some Zuñi clans say their clan ancestors migrated to their present location from central Arizona. But as far back as the beginning of the Great Pueblo period this was home for peoples inhabiting the Village of the Great Kivas and a score and more of other large pueblos.

The peak of building activity came during the fourteenth and fifteenth centuries. With peoples moving in from other parts of Arizona and New Mexico, large pueblos similar to those of the Hopi country were built. One of the largest and best known of these was Hawikuh, a big two- and three-story structure dating back to the fourteenth century. Early kivas, like those in the Village of the Great Kivas, were circular, but in later periods they became rectangular.

Like all their neighbors, the early Zuñi peoples manufactured black-on-white pots. Later, they began making redware, with decoration in black and then in both black and white. Either these Zuñi Indians or some of their relatives to the west even introduced a new fad in decoration, glaze paint made from ores that had lead in them. When fired, this new paint had a glossy or shiny appearance. Lighter backgrounds came back into style, with designs in black, purplish-black, or greenish glaze paint.

A hundred miles east of the Zuñi country lies the valley of the Rio Grande, the last of the new centers of population. During earlier periods the Rio Grande was far removed from the Pueblo world of the Four Corners country. Its first villages seem to have been founded by outcasts or refugees from the western pueblos. Being on the outskirts of civilization, as it were, it lagged behind the west in architecture and in arts and industries.

But by the end of the thirteenth century and the opening of the fourteenth, when more and more refugees moved into the valley, business picked up fast. What the west lost, the east gained. Small to large pueblos sprang up all along the upper Rio Grande Valley and on the plateaus bordering the valley.

Up in Rito de los Frijoles Canyon, Spanish for "bean creek," some bands of refugee Cliff Dwellers even found cliffs of relatively soft volcanic ash. They gouged out holes in these and made small cave rooms. Against the foot of the cliffs they constructed terraced houses from one to three stories in height. Some of these villages extend along the base of the cliff for nearly two miles.

But most of the Rio Grande villages were located out in the open, either on low mesas or in the valleys. Pueblos were generally rectangular in shape, built around open courtyards, and were from one to four stories in height. Walls were sometimes of adobe alone, sometimes of stone laid in adobe mortar.

Although most kivas were circular and subterranean, there were some square or rectangular aboveground kivas. These square kivas seem to have been later than the round, perhaps coming in from the Zuñi area. Rio Grande kivas lacked the benches and pillars or pilasters so common in western kivas.

Well into the 1300's most Rio Grande pueblos were relatively small, from 50 to 100 or more rooms. Then they

Fig. 61. Terraced cliff village in Bandelier National Monument, New Mexico.

began to lessen in number and increase in size, many ranging up to 800 rooms. One of the largest during this period was Pecos Pueblo, located east of the Rio Grande River on the headwaters of the Pecos River.

Pecos was founded about 1300 A.D., one of a number of similar small villages out on the edge of the plains. Gradually, as nomadic Indian tribes pushed into New Mexico from the north and east, the smaller pueblos were abandoned, their inhabitants seeking refuge at Pecos. By the opening of the fifteenth century Pecos was the last pueblo remaining on the eastern frontier. By the end of that century it had grown into a terraced, four-story, rectangular structure surrounding a large courtyard.

At Pecos and the other Rio Grande pueblos black-on-white was the earliest decorated pottery. But it was soon replaced by pots with a gray or tan background and designs in black. Some time after 1300 glaze paint was introduced from the west and quickly became the fashion. Glaze paint was first used to decorate redware, as it had been in the west. But it wasn't long before light-colored backgrounds began to be used. Vessels were generally decorated in two or three colors.

Although a few troughed metates have been found in early Rio Grande villages, most grinding stones were of the so-called flat type. Strangely enough very few have ever been found in place in mealing bins. Perhaps this is because only ground-floor rooms remain intact in most pueblos. These rooms would have been too dark for any use except storage. Probably such bins were located in the upper row of rooms where it was lighter.

The three-quarter grooved, Hohokam-type stone ax never reached the Rio Grande pueblos. In the early periods the standard ax was the full-grooved Anasazi form. After glaze painting appeared in the fourteenth century, a new variety of ax was developed. This was a well-made, spiral-grooved ax, one in which the flexible wooden haft was wrapped twice about the ax head.

Throughout the Rio Grande area most burials were flexed. At the large fifteenth-century pueblo of Unshagi, for example, out of 162 recorded burials only ten were extended full length. Bodies were usually wrapped in mats or blankets or cloth or hide. Buffalo hide was used at some of the eastern pueblos close to the plains. Grave offerings were, as a rule, not as numerous as they had been in contemporary graves in the west. At Pecos nearly 2,000 burials were found in abandoned rooms and in trash mounds. Yet the Pecos people were not extravagant when it came to leaving gifts for the dead. Only 573 contained decorated pottery, and there was generally only one piece to a grave. And ornaments of any kind were rare.

By the opening of the sixteenth century the Pueblo Indian world had contracted into three centers — the Hopi in northern Arizona, the Zuñi in western New Mexico, and the Rio Grande in north central New Mexico. Of all the hundreds of cliff dwellings and pueblos inhabited during the preceding period, there were only some seventy left. All the rest of what had been Pueblo territory was either empty or the home of scattered bands of nomadic Indian tribes.

# 13
# The
# Spanish Invasion

On July 7, 1540, the residents of the Zuñi town of Hawikuh were startled by the sudden appearance of a horde of white-faced men wearing shiny breastplates and helmets and mounted on huge four-footed animals. Francisco Vásquez de Coronado and his advance guard of Spanish soldiers and Mexican Indian attendants had arrived to begin the conquest of the land of the Pueblos.

The surprise of the Zuñi Indians was no greater than that of the Spaniards. They had been hunting for cities of gold and had, instead, found only a stone and mud village, with no gold, no silver, no jewels except turquoise.

After Cortez conquered the Aztecs and other Indian tribes of Mexico in 1520 and Pizarro took care of the Incas of Peru a dozen years later, the Spaniards began looking around for more rich Indian civilizations to liberate. In 1536 an answer to their prayers turned up in Cabeza de Vaca and three other half-naked Spaniards. They were the survivors of an ill-fated expedition to Florida in 1528. On their almost incredible journey across the southern part of the continent to Mexico they had picked up strange stories of rich Indian cities far to the north.

Similar tales had already filtered down into Mexico, tales of terraced towns whose streets were paved with gold and whose houses were studded with jewels. There were seven of these fabulous cities, the famed "Seven Cities of Cibola." The eager Spanish adventurers, who had just got through plundering the Aztecs, Mayas, and Incas of their gold and silver and jade, now had these tales confirmed by Cabeza de Vaca's account. Even richer cities lay up there to the north waiting to be discovered.

In 1539 a Franciscan friar, Marcos de Niza, and Esteban, an African or Moorish slave who had been with Cabeza de Vaca, went north to investigate the rumors. De Niza sent Esteban on ahead with an escort of Mexican Indians. Esteban seems to have reached Hawikuh where he was presently killed, together with several of his followers. Learning of this from the survivors, Marcos de Niza returned to Mexico, but not before he had supposedly viewed Hawikuh from a safe distance.

His slightly exaggerated story that he had glimpsed a city far larger than Mexico City was enough to stir the Spaniards into action. Coronado and his army promptly headed north. To say they were disappointed in what they found is putting it mildly. Here was no wealthy city to be robbed, only a town of simple farmers to whom riches meant nothing.

The Zuñis didn't like the attitude of their guests and put up a stubborn resistance. But their bows and arrows were no match for armor and guns and horses, and Hawikuh was captured. The Zuñis took refuge in the hills and Coronado and his men settled down in the town to rest from their long journey northward.

Hearing of a land called Tusayan to the northwest, Coronado sent Don Pedro de Tovar and twenty soldiers to look into it. The Spaniards caught the Hopis by surprise at the pueblo of Awatovi and quickly subdued them. The Hopis told Tovar of a large river to the west. When he reported this to Coronado, the latter sent out another expedition under Captain García López de Cárdenas. Again visiting the Hopi villages and securing guides, Cárdenas went on to discover the Grand Canyon of the Colorado and become that national park's first tourist.

Learning of still more towns to the east of Hawikuh and the half dozen other Zuñi villages, Coronado, still hoping to find treasure, sent out Hernando de Alvarado and twenty soldiers. Alvarado discovered Acoma and the pueblo of Tiguex on the Rio Grande and went on east as far as Pecos. This he described as a big village four stories high built on a rock. He sent back word to Coronado that the Rio Grande Valley would be a good place to winter. As soon as the rest of the army had reached Hawikuh, Coronado moved on to Tiguex where they spent the next few months.

Trouble wasn't long in developing. Feeding, housing, and clothing an army of 300 Spanish soldiers and some 800 Mexican Indian followers, not to mention over 500 horses and an unknown number of cattle, sheep, and swine, was a gigantic task for the Pueblo Indians. On top of this the Spaniards were overbearing, taking hostages right and left and demanding more than could be provided. The Indians stood the injustices as long as they could and finally revolted. The Spaniards hunted down and killed many of them and laid siege to the pueblo of Tiguex. Before the war was over several hundred Indians had been massacred.

During the winter the Spaniards had been regaled by the

Fig. 62. Tyuonyi Pueblo in Bandelier National Monument,
New Mexico.

tales of an imaginative eastern Plains Indian, a captive at Pecos. This Indian, called Turk by the Spaniards, told them of the land of Quivira to the northeast, a wonderful land of gold and silver. Coronado couldn't resist the lure. In the spring he and his army set out across the plains, with Turk guiding them. After months of wandering through Texas and Oklahoma, they finally reached the mythical land of Quivira somewhere in Kansas. Since the Indian villages they found were even poorer than those of the Pueblo Indians, Coronado had Turk killed for his treachery and returned to the Rio Grande. After further explorations up and down the river, visiting Jemez and Taos and other pueblos, Coronado and his army left for Mexico in the spring of 1542.

Two Franciscan friars elected to remain behind, one at Quivira and one at Pecos. As might be expected, they were both martyred within a very short time. The band of sheep that had been left behind with the friar at Pecos probably didn't last much longer.

Coronado took back with him no gold or silver, no precious jewels. As far as the Spaniards were concerned, the expedition had been a failure. They had found no magnificent cities, no fabulous treasures. They were glad to get back to Mexico with their skins intact.

Yet to today's archaeologists the expedition was of extreme importance. From the written accounts kept by Castaneda, the chronicler of the expedition, we get our first detailed description of the pueblos and the people who lived in them. The Pueblo Indians now emerge from the shadowy realm of prehistory into the full light of history. We can locate exactly many of the towns and places the Spaniards visited. They didn't discover every pueblo in the Southwest.

Such large towns as Tyuonyi in Frijoles Canyon and Puye on the plateau above were not mentioned in the chronicles. Both seem to have been abandoned shortly after Coronado's departure.

The Pueblo Indians were equally happy to see the Spaniards head back for Mexico. They didn't want any part of these white-faced strangers or their unearthly weapons or their religion. All the Indians wanted was to be left alone. They hoped they had seen the last of the Spaniards.

They had, for a time. It was nearly 40 years before they saw their next Spaniard. Beginning in 1581, over the next decade at least three different exploring expeditions toured New Mexico and Arizona. The first party left three Franciscans behind to convert the Indians. The following expedition learned that all three had been killed. These brief visits had little real effect on the Pueblos. In between they went on about their farming, their social life, and their ceremonies as they had for centuries.

But in 1598 the Spaniards came back, this time to stay. Juan de Oñate brought with him not only 129 soldiers but also nearly 300 settlers, 83 wagons, and 7,000 head of cattle, horses, and sheep. There were also eight or ten missionaries to convert the heathen. Oñate quickly brought most of the Indian pueblos under his control. Only with Acoma did he have any difficulty and that supposedly impregnable sky city was soon captured and many of its inhabitants slaughtered. Beside San Juan Pueblo on the Rio Grande, Oñate established the first Spanish settlement in New Mexico. In 1609 Santa Fe was founded and became the capital of New Spain.

In 1605, on returning from an exploration trip to the Colorado River, Oñate camped at a spring on the trail between Zuñi and Acoma. Towering 200 feet above the

spring was a huge sandstone cliff, called El Morro by the
Spaniards. Prehistoric Indians had pecked in the soft rock
hundreds of drawings or petroglyphs. Oñate continued this
practice, carving his name and the date, April 16, 1605.
Other seventeenth- and eighteenth-century Spanish travelers added their names and dates beside Oñate's. The last
Spanish inscription was made in 1774. But the nineteenth
century brought American explorers and soldiers and traders who also left their records inscribed in the rock. Now
Inscription Rock is preserved as a national monument.

From the very beginning the Spaniards and the Pueblo
Indians didn't get along any too well. The Spaniards, from
the soldiers to the settlers to the missionaries, looked upon
the Indians as a conquered people, to be treated as subjects,
slaves, servants. Everyone exploited the Indians. Most governors and other officials looked upon their positions as an
opportunity to enrich themselves. This meant using the
Indians in any and every way possible and exacting tribute
in corn and cloth. The settlers wanted free labor in building houses and tilling fields.

The missionaries tried to stamp out native religious beliefs and practices, forcibly if necessary. To accomplish
this they built great churches in many of the pueblos, using,
of course, Indian labor. They kept herds of cattle and sheep,
using Indians as herders. They introduced wheat and watermelons and peppers and peaches, using Indian labor to farm
their church fields.

The Spaniards tried to impose their own form of government upon the Indians. The village chiefs became governors,
sub-chiefs, alcaldes. Yet the elders and society leaders were
still strong and the native priests still had charge of native
rituals and ceremonies.

The Pueblo Indians learned how to grow wheat and

peaches and watermelons. But they still raised corn in the old ways and still ground it on stone metates. They learned to use burros as beasts of burden. They added wool to their native cotton, but the men still continued to be the weavers, working in the kivas as their ancestors had done. Most of the Indians became Catholics, in name at least. But they did not give up their kivas or their native religion.

Added to the troubles of the Pueblos was the increasing pressure of nomadic Indian tribes. Several times we have mentioned the possibility of nomadic Indians' raiding the pueblos in earlier periods. But we always ended up by saying there was no definite proof of such nomads. Now we have that proof. As early as 1541 Spanish documents indicate such Indians in eastern New Mexico. In 1598 Oñate used the world Apache for the first time.

The half dozen different Apache tribes, together with their close relatives, the Navaho, came originally from Canada, where other relatives still live. They reached the Southwest some time between the thirteenth and sixteenth centuries. From Spanish records we know they were in New Mexico in the 1500's. Beyond that we can't say.

Strangely enough, most of the early Spanish accounts about the Apache Indians speak not of raids but of trading activities between the Pueblos and the nomads.

To some extent there was justification for many of the Apache Indian raids on the Spaniards. The Spaniards saw in the nomadic Indian tribes a rich source of slave material. Many officials sent out regular expeditions after Indian slaves, frequently using Pueblo Indians as slave catchers. It is known that one Spanish governor had some ninety Apache slaves.

Naturally the Apaches resented this and in turn started plundering Spaniards and Pueblos alike. When the Apaches began acquiring horses, stolen from the Spaniards, they were able to extend their raiding over a much wider area. By 1669 one Spanish writer reported that persons traveled only at the risk of their lives, that no road was safe from attack by the heathen Apache. Seven years later conditions hadn't improved. A petition was sent to Mexico asking for reinforcements to fight off Apache raiders.

In the meanwhile, time hadn't improved relations between the Spaniards and the Pueblo Indians. If anything, they were growing worse. Franciscan attempts to wipe out native religion caused the most friction between the two groups. Indians who wouldn't give up their religion were whipped, imprisoned, sold into slavery, and even hanged. This didn't help the situation. On top of this each new governor, and there were many of them, seemed to impose heavier and heavier taxes of corn and cotton cloth on the Indians. Year by year hostility increased. From 1640 to 1680 there were half a dozen different Pueblo revolts against their masters. But the Indians were never organized, only a few towns taking part at any one time, and the Spaniards were easily able to subdue them.

Then came the Pueblo revolt of 1680. Historians have called this the first American revolution. Like the revolution of our own ancestors against the British a hundred years later, this was also successful. For the first and only time in their history, all of the pueblos united together, even the distant Hopi towns in Arizona. Under the leadership of Popé, a medicine man of San Juan Pueblo, an elaborate plan was drawn up. Popé sent a knotted cord around to all the pueblos, each knot representing a day remaining before that set for the attack, August 13, 1860.

But there were too many in on the secret. The news leaked out. The Spaniards, however, had heard the cry of wolf too often in recent years and didn't heed the warning. When they finally woke up to the fact that this was no joke, it was already too late. Some four hundred Spaniards were killed and the rest forced all the way back to what is now El Paso, Texas.

The Pueblo Indians celebrated their victory by tearing down the churches, burning ranches and farms, and destroying all other signs of the hated Spaniards.

For the next twelve years the Indians managed to keep the Spaniards out of the country. But in 1692 Diego de Vargas reconquered the Pueblos without firing a shot. His task was made easy because the Indians were no longer united. They hadn't stayed together very long after the revolt.

The Pueblo Indians never did form a single tribe with a single language. Each pueblo was separate from all the others, speaking only one of half a dozen different languages. Each had its own government, its own religious leaders, its own clan system, and, in a general sense, its own distinctive ways of making and doing things. Popé had somehow managed to unite them once, but he couldn't do it a second time. Success went to his head and he tried to become a dictator. The democratic Pueblos would have nothing to do with this and went back to being individual towns again. Divided, one by one they buckled under to Vargas's show of force.

Drastic changes took place among the Pueblo Indians in the years just before and after the revolt of 1680 and the reconquest of 1692. In one way or another wars, disease, Spaniards, and nomadic Indians forced the abandonment of scores of towns. In 1540, there had been some seventy pueblos in Arizona and New Mexico. By 1700, there were only twenty-five or thirty left. Some of these were new towns that had been founded in more easily defended spots by people who had deserted their former villages.

One such was the Hopi town of Walpi. Old Walpi had been located near the foot of a high mesa. About 1700, fearing attack by the Spaniards, the inhabitants moved their pueblo several hundred feet straight up to the top of the mesa where it still stands today.

Some Pueblo Indians hated the Spaniards so much that they moved in with the Navaho Indians in northern New Mexico. There they stayed for nearly half a century.

The Spaniards wasted no time in again clamping their iron-fisted rule over the Pueblos. The Franciscans began reconverting the Indians, churches were rebuilt, new ranches established, and more farm lands cleared.

But there was one Pueblo region the Spaniards never reoccupied. That was the Hopi country. The Hopis put up no resistance to the reconquest, but only at Awatovi were missionaries allowed. So strong was the Hopi feeling against the foreign religion that in 1700 the other Hopi towns got

Fig. 63. Hopi town of Walpi on top of First Mesa, northern Arizona.

together and sacked Awatovi, killing the men and distributing the women and children among the various towns. Over the next fifty years the Spaniards sent out at least eight expeditions, but they could never regain their hold over the Hopis.

The Hopi mesas even became a refuge for other Pueblo rebels. Although most of these people eventually drifted back to their homelands in the east, one group of Rio Grande Indians stayed. Around 1700 they built their own town of Hano right next to Walpi and live there today, still speaking their own distinct language.

All during the eighteenth century the Spanish settlements and missions had to fight off repeated attacks from raiding bands of Navaho, Apache, and Comanche Indians. Many of the pueblos also suffered from these raids.

Pecos, standing all alone on the eastern frontier, had been the biggest of the pueblos. But by 1750, due largely to Comanche raids, its population had fallen to 450. The census of 1790 could count only 154 Pecos residents. In 1838 the seventeen survivors gave it up as a bad job and moved to Jemez Pueblo, leaving the once mighty town to fall into ruins.

In the nineteenth century the Pueblo Indians changed masters twice. In 1821 Mexico won her freedom from Spain and, twenty-seven years later, in 1848, the United States took over control of Arizona and New Mexico. The second of these events opened the door for a flood of Americans — soldiers, traders, merchants, farmers, miners, cattlemen, and Protestant missionaries. Their coming opened a new era for the Indians.

# 14
# Pueblo
# Indians Today

In spite of 400 years of exposure to Spanish, Mexican, and American civilization, Pueblo culture has changed relatively little. Today most of the Pueblo Indians live much as their ancestors did in 1540.

Many still build terraced apartment houses several stories high. All of the modern pueblos have their ceremonial chambers, their kivas. Some are round and some are rectangular. Although most are now aboveground, some are still subterranean. But they perform the same function as they did in ancient times. They are still social and work rooms for the men and also serve as council chambers. In them are put on rituals and ceremonies which have been handed down from generation to generation.

Each pueblo is still independent from all others. Each has its own governing council, its own clans and secret societies, its own special ritual dances and ceremonies, its own farming lands.

Most of the Pueblo Indians still make beautifully decorated pottery. As in the past, each village has its unique vessel shapes and styles of design. Some still make basketry.

Some still make turquoise and other fine jewelry. Weaving is still thought to be man's work and is still usually done on looms set up in the kivas.

Most Pueblo Indians are still farmers, raising corn, beans, and squash in small gardens just as their ancestors did. Metates and manos are still considered as standard items of household equipment.

Pueblo architecture, agriculture, ceremonial practices, and social systems may have changed little over the centuries. But numerous other changes have gradually worked their way into the lives of these people.

Outwardly at least, most of the younger generation attempt to look and dress like their white neighbors. Only among the older or more conservative people can you still find the old-style colorful blankets and blanket dresses, breechcloths, and moccasins. Machine-made fabrics are replacing native-made cloth.

Pottery is still commonly used for cooking and for storage of drinking water. But most of the pottery manufactured today is for sale to tourists, its place in the home being taken by metal pans and china dishes. Only at a few pueblos is basketry still made and most of that is also for sale. The same holds true for turquoise jewelry.

Most of the Indians now keep livestock of one kind or another and most also raise fruits and vegetables acquired from the Spanish and the Americans. They use metal tools and machinery for cultivating their fields. Burros and horses and wagons are being replaced by trucks and cars.

Although basic architecture hasn't changed, the houses aren't the same as they were even fifty years ago. Most of them now have wooden doors and glass windows. Single, detached houses are going up in some villages. Many towns

Fig. 64. Modern Zuñi Pueblo in western New Mexico.

have electricity and a great many houses have such modern appliances as refrigerators, freezers, washing machines, radios, and television sets. At least one pueblo has its own sewer system. The inhabitants of Zuñi installed a water system to pipe water into their homes. Several others have done the same.

Of all the pueblos the Hopi towns have been least affected by these changes. After the revolt of 1680 they were never reoccupied by the Spaniards and the desert country in which they are located was too uninviting and too hard to reach to attract later Spanish or American settlers.

Today the 600,000-acre Hopi reservation is completely surrounded by the much larger Navaho Indian Reservation. On three high barren mesas perch the ten or eleven surviving Hopi towns. In them live some 4,000 Hopi Indians.

Oraibi, on the third or westernmost mesa, is the oldest and the most famous of the Hopi pueblos. Up until 1906 it was also the largest. But in that year the inhabitants split

Fig. 65. Hopi Indian chief at Oraibi Pueblo, Arizona.

into two factions, conservatives and liberals. The conservative party was against the federal government, the schools, the missions, and whites in general. The liberals were willing to compromise. To settle the dispute the two sides engaged in a push-of-war, the losing side to leave the pueblo. The liberals won by pushing the conservatives across a line drawn in the sand. The defeated conservatives, some 300 to 400 in number, packed up their belongings and left the same day, founding the town of Hotevilla 8 miles away on the same mesa top.

Some of the less conservative members later tried to return to Oraibi. But they were again driven out and founded the village of Bakavi not far from Hotevilla. Oraibi's population was still further depleted by migrations to the summer colony of Moencopi 40 miles to the west. About 1910 the town of New Oraibi sprang up at the foot of the mesa, even further reducing the population. Yet today several hundred Hopis still live in the partially ruined pueblo.

Among the Hopis, as with the other Pueblo Indians, religion was and still is the center of their existence. Around it revolve all other features of their life — their hunting and gathering, their agricultural activities, their building, their pottery and basketry making, their social and political system. The Hopis have extremely elaborate and numerous rites and ceremonies. Most of the ceremonies last either nine or seventeen days, the first eight or sixteen days being taken up with secret rituals and prayers. Part of these secret rites take place in the underground kivas. Their most famous and unusual ceremony is the Snake Dance, performed each year in August to bring rain for their crops. Now that the Hopi mesas can be reached by a paved road, no visitor to the Southwest should miss seeing this colorful ceremony.

Here, like the archaeologist, you can still catch your archaeology alive. Oraibi dates back 700 and more years into the Pueblo Golden Age. Present-day Walpi and Shongopovi and Mishongnovi go back at least to the time of the Pueblo Revolt, and several others have nearly as long a history.

On First Mesa the Hopi women still make fine pottery, with black or red bird and feather designs on a cream or yellow background. On Second Mesa they weave coiled baskets and on Third Mesa beautiful wicker plaques.

Southeast of the Hopi country, just over the border in New Mexico, is the pueblo of Zuñi. There were six or seven Zuñi towns when Coronado arrived in 1540, but they were all abandoned before or during the Pueblo Revolt. Now there is only Zuñi itself, established about 1695 near one of the abandoned pueblos, and a few summer camps or farming villages.

Zuñi and Hopi, the two westernmost of the pueblos, are sometimes called the Desert Pueblos. They have always traded back and forth and have many of the same customs. But their inhabitants speak totally different languages. Zuñi pottery is also different from that of the Hopi. Black and red designs, often of deer or long-tailed birds, are painted on a white background. In recent years Zuñi silversmiths have become famous for their fine jewelry.

Midway between the Desert Dwellers and the Rio Grande are two other pueblos, Acoma and Laguna. Acoma stands on top of a 400-foot-high mesa. It is one of the older towns, occupying the same location it did when the Spaniards first came. Laguna, a few miles to the east, is newer, founded just after the Pueblo Revolt by refugees from the Rio Grande. The inhabitants of these two towns speak Keresan, the language of five other pueblos along the Rio Grande.

Up and down the Rio Grande Valley, from Taos 70 miles north of Santa Fe to Isleta 12 miles south of Albuquerque, are the sixteen present-day River Pueblos. By language, these fall into four groups. The members of five pueblos, Zia, Santa Ana, San Felipe, Santo Domingo, and Cochiti, speak Keresan, the same language as do their relatives at Acoma and Laguna.

All of the other pueblos belong to one language division, the Tanoan, but this in turn is divided into three languages which are not intelligible to one another. At Santa Clara, San Ildefonso, San Juan, Nambe, Pojoaque, and Tesuque the Tewa language is spoken. It is also spoken by the residents of Hano in the Hopi country. The people of Taos, Picuris, Sandia, and Isleta speak dialects of Tiwa. The last pueblo, Jemez, is the only one today in which the Towa language is used.

Like their western cousins, the inhabitants of most of the Rio Grande pueblos also make pottery. In general, each pueblo has its traditional patterns and forms. The women of San Juan, Santa Clara, and San Ildefonso are noted for their polished red and polished black pottery. About forty years ago several potters at San Ildefonso began to make highly polished black jars with designs in dull black. This style became so popular that it has spread to other pueblos.

Unlike the Hopi towns, these New Mexico pueblos are not on reservations. The Hopi were never actually under Spanish control and thus never received land from the Spanish government. Not until 1882 was a reservation set aside for them by the United States government.

But the New Mexican pueblos are on land which was granted to them by the Spanish Crown nearly 300 years ago. These grants were later confirmed and guaranteed by the

United States Congress. These Pueblo Indians are among the few Indian groups in the United States who have title to their land, instead of living on land owned by the federal government and reserved for Indian use.

The Pueblo Indians are slowly increasing in numbers. Today there are some 25,000 of them living in thirty-odd towns and villages in Arizona and New Mexico.

The Atomic Age has come to the Southwest. Railroads and highways crisscross the desert and mountains; giant planes leave vapor trails across the blue sky. Cities and towns are spreading out over the countryside. But all these signs of progress have touched the Pueblo Indian only lightly. Life still goes on in the ancient pueblos much as it did a thousand years ago. Painted and masked dancers still perform their age-old ceremonies in the kivas. The Pueblo Indian rests serene in the knowledge that he is still living in the center of the universe, that his own gods still rule over his world.

# Bibliography

Amsden, Charles Avery. *Prehistoric Southwesterners From Basketmakers to Pueblo.* Los Angeles: Southwest Museum, 1949.

Baldwin, Gordon C. *America's Buried Past.* New York: G. P. Putnam's Sons, 1962.

———. *The World of Prehistory.* New York: G. P. Putnam's Sons, 1963.

———. *The Warrior Apache.* Globe, Arizona: Dale Stuart King Publisher, 1963.

Cummings, Byron. *First Inhabitants of Arizona and the Southwest.* Tucson, Arizona: Cummings Publication Council, 1953.

Douglas, Frederic H., and D'Harnoncourt, René. *Indian Art of the United States.* New York: The Museum of Modern Art, 1941.

Douglass, A. E. *Dating Pueblo Bonito and Other Ruins of the Southwest.* Washington, D.C.: National Geographic Society, 1935.

Dutton, Bertha, (ed.). *Indians of the Southwest.* Santa Fe, New Mexico: New Mexico Association on Indian Affairs, 1958.

Gilpin, Laura. *The Pueblos: A Camera Chronicle.* New York: Hastings House, 1941.

Josephy, A. M., Jr. (ed.). *The American Heritage Book of Indians.* New York: American Heritage Publishing Co., 1961.

Judd, Neil M. *The Material Culture of Pueblo Bonito.* (Smith-

213

sonian Institution Miscellaneous Collections, Vol. 124.) Washington, D.C.: 1954.

Kidder, Alfred Vincent. *An Introduction to the Study of Southwestern Archaeology*. New Haven, Conn.: Yale University Press, 1962.

Lancaster, James A.; Pinkley, Jean M.; Van Cleave, Philip F.; and Watson, Don. *Archeological Excavations in Mesa Verde National Park, Colorado, 1950*. (National Park Service Archaeological Research Series No. 2.) Washington, D.C.: 1954.

McGregor, John C. *Southwestern Archaeology*. New York: John Wiley & Sons, 1941.

Marriott, Alice. *Maria: The Potter of San Ildefonso*. Norman, Oklahoma: University of Oklahoma Press, 1948.

Martin, Paul S.; Quimby, George I.; and Collier, Donald. *Indians Before Columbus*. Chicago: University of Chicago Press, 1947.

Morris, Anne Axtell. *Digging in the Southwest*. New York: Doubleday, Doran & Co., 1933.

Roberts, Frank H. H., Jr. *The Village of the Great Kivas on the Zuñi Reservation, New Mexico*. (Smithsonian Institution, Bureau of American Ethnology Bulletin 111.) Washington, D.C.: 1932.

Spicer, Edward H. *Cycles of Conquest*. Tucson, Arizona: University of Arizona Press, 1962.

Stubbs, Stanley A. *Bird's-Eye View of the Pueblos*. Norman, Oklahoma: University of Oklahoma Press, 1950.

Underhill, Ruth. *First Penthouse Dwellers of America*. Santa Fe, New Mexico: Laboratory of Anthropology, 1947.

———. *Red Man's America*. Chicago: University of Chicago Press, 1953.

Watson, Don. *Indians of the Mesa Verde*. Mesa Verde National Park, Colorado: Mesa Verde Museum Association, 1953.

Wormington, H. M. *Prehistoric Indians of the Southwest*. Denver: The Denver Museum of Natural History, 1947.

Wormington, H. M., and Neal, Arminta. *The Story of Pueblo Pottery*. Denver: The Denver Museum of Natural History, 1951.

# Glossary

ADOBE — Clay used by some southwestern Indians in building houses.

ANASAZI — Navaho Indian word, meaning "the ancient ones," referring to the prehistoric Cliff Dweller and Pueblo Indians.

ARCHAEOLOGY — The scientific study of the material remains of ancient peoples.

ARTIFACT — Archaeological term for any object made by man.

ATLATL — Aztec Indian word for the spear thrower used by many prehistoric people to hurl darts or spears.

AWL — A pointed tool, usually of bone, used to pierce hides or other materials.

BASKETMAKER — A prehistoric group of Indians living in the Four Corners area nearly 2,000 years ago.

CIST — A circular or oval pit, sometimes slab-lined, used by the Basketmakers and other peoples for storage.

CLAN — A social organization common to many primitive or early people, clan membership depending upon whether descent is reckoned on the mother's or father's side.

CLIFF DWELLERS — Prehistoric Pueblo Indians who lived in houses built in caves in the cliffs.

CORRUGATED POTTERY — Pottery in which the coils have been pinched together to form ridges.

215

CULTURE — An archaeological term for the tools and other remains showing how a particular group of people lived.

DENDROCHRONOLOGY — A method of dating prehistoric ruins by the annual rings in certain trees.

HOHOKAM — The Pima Indian word for the prehistoric inhabitants of southern Arizona.

KACHINAS — Masked impersonations of supernatural beings in Pueblo Indian religion.

KIVA — The ceremonial chamber of the Pueblo Indians.

MANO — A hand stone used for grinding.

METATE — The stone slab on which a mano is rubbed to grind corn or other materials.

MOGOLLON — An early agricultural, pottery-making culture in eastern Arizona and western New Mexico.

PATAYAN — A prehistoric culture along the Colorado River in western Arizona and extreme eastern California.

PETROGLYPHS — Also called pictographs, these are designs carved or pecked or painted on rock.

POLYCHROME POTTERY — Pottery decorated with more than two colors.

POTSHERD — A fragment of broken pottery.

PROJECTILE POINT — An arrowhead, spearhead, or dart point.

PUEBLO — The Spanish word for town, used by archaeologists to refer to Indian stone and adobe community houses and their inhabitants.

SALADO — A group of prehistoric Indians in eastern and southern Arizona.

SINAGUA — A group of prehistoric Indians formerly living in the vicinity of Flagstaff, Arizona.

SITE — Any place that shows evidence of human occupation such as potsherds, broken stone tools, fragments of walls, etc.

# The
# Author

Gordon C. Baldwin has been deeply involved in anthropology, the study of man, since his undergraduate days at the University of Arizona more than thirty years ago. While his studies have been wide-ranging, his special area of interest is the ancient Indian cultures of the Southwest.

He has been an instructor in archaeology, a branch of anthropology, at the University of Arizona; curator of the Arizona State Museum; an archaeologist with the National Park Service; director of archaeological survey and salvage work for the National Park Service in areas where flood control projects threatened to destroy evidence of ancient men. He received his doctorate from the University of Southern California.

For many years he contributed articles to various special scientific journals, but in 1954 he found he had a talent for writing more popular material and ultimately published eight successful adult western novels. In 1960 he was pursuaded to combine his special knowledge and writing ability to tell younger readers about his exciting field of work, which is too often obscured by technical language. The result was *America's Buried Past*, published in 1962, and the present book. Two others are in preparation.

Dr. Baldwin lives with his wife in Tucson, Arizona. He has two daughters and three grandchildren.

# Index

219